THE RICHEST MAN IN BABYLON

The Richest Man
in
Babylon

George S. Clason

THE RICHEST MAN in Babylon had a system which led him to the goal he desired.

In this book he tells his system—gives it to us to follow without cost or obligation.

His system is recommended to every person desiring to arrive at that same goal, *financial plenty*.

The Richest Man In Babylon

Tells His System

By

GEORGE S. CLASON

First published in 1926 as separate pamphlets by
George S. Clason

Reprint edition by Sound Wisdom, 2018.

ISBN 13 TP: 978-1-64095-049-8

13 / 22 21

Contents

"If you have not acquired more than a bare existence since ye were youths, it is because you either have failed to learn the laws that govern the building of wealth, or else you do not observe them."

The Richest Man In Babylon

Tells His System

IN Old Babylon there once lived a certain very rich man named Arkad. Far and wide he was famed for his great wealth. Also was he famed for his liberality. He was generous in his charities. He was generous with his family. He was liberal in his own expenses. But nevertheless each year his wealth increased more rapidly than he spent it.

And there were certain friends of younger days who came to him and said: "You, Arkad, are more fortunate than we. You have become the richest man in all Babylon while we struggle for existence. You can wear the finest garments and you can enjoy the rarest foods, while we must be content if we can clothe our families in raiment that is presentable and feed them as best we can.

"Yet, once we were equal. We studied under the same master. We played in the same games. And in neither the studies nor the games did you outshine us. And in the years since, you have been no more an honorable citizen than we.

"Nor, have you worked harder or more faithfully, in so far as we can judge. Why, then, should a fickle fate single you out to enjoy all the good things of life and ignore us who are equally deserving?"

Thereupon Arkad remonstrated with them, saying, "If you have not acquired more than a bare existence in the years since we were youths, it is because you either have failed to learn the laws that govern the building of wealth, or else you do not observe them.

"'Fickle fate' is a vicious goddess that brings no permanent good to anyone. On the contrary, she brings ruin to almost every man upon whom she showers unearned gold. She makes wanton spenders, who soon dissipate all they receive and are left beset by overwhelming appetites and desires they have not the ability to gratify. Yet others whom she favors become misers and hoard their wealth, fearing to spend what they have, knowing they do not possess the ability to replace it. They further are beset by fear of robbers and doom themselves to lives of emptiness and secret misery.

"Others, there probably are, who can take unearned gold and add to it and continue to be happy and contented citizens. But so few are they, I know of them but by hearsay. Think you of the men who have inherited sudden wealth and see if these things are not so."

His friends admitted that of the men they knew who had inherited wealth these words were true, and they besought him to explain to them how he had become possessed of so much property, so he continued:

"In my youth I looked about me and saw all the good things there were to bring happiness and contentment. And I realized that wealth increased the potency of all these.

"Wealth is a power. With wealth many things are possible.

"One may ornament the home with the richest of furnishings.

"One may sail the distant seas.

"One may feast on the delicacies of far lands.

"One may buy the ornaments of the gold worker and the stone polisher.

"One may even build mighty temples for the gods.

"One may do all these things and many others in which there is delight for the senses and gratification for the soul.

"And when I realized all this I declared to myself that I would claim my share of the good things of life. I would not be one of those who stand afar off, enviously watching others enjoy. I would not be content to clothe myself in the cheapest raiment that looked respectable. I would not be satisfied with the lot of a poor man. On the contrary I would make myself a guest at this banquet of good things.

"Being, as you know, the son of an humble merchant, one of a large family with no hope of an inheritance, and not being endowed, as you have so frankly said, with superior powers or wisdom, I decided that if I was to achieve what I desired, time and study would be required.

"As for time, all men have it in abundance. You, each of you, have let slip by sufficient to have made yourselves wealthy. Yet, you admit you have nothing to show except your good families, of which you can be justly proud.

"As for study, did not our wise teacher teach us that learning was of two kinds: the one kind being the things we learned and knew, and the other being in the training that taught us how to find out what we did not know?

"Therefore, did I decide to find out how one might accumulate wealth, and when I had found out, to make this my task and do it well. For is it not wise that we should enjoy while we dwell in the brightness of the sunshine? For sorrows enough shall descend upon us when we depart for the darkness of the world of spirit.

"I found employment as a scribe in the hall of records, and long hours each day I labored upon the clay tablets. Week after week, and month after month, I labored, yet for my earnings I had naught to show. Food and clothing and penance to the gods, and other things of which I could remember not what, absorbed all my earnings. But my determination did not leave me.

"And one day Algamish the money lender, came to the house of the city master and ordered a copy of the Ninth Law, and he said to me, 'I must have this in two days, and if the task is done by that time, two coppers will I give thee.'

"So I labored hard, but the law was long, and when Algamish returned the task was unfinished.

He was angry, and had I been his slave he would have beaten me. But knowing the city master would not permit him to injure me, I was unafraid, so I said to him:

"'Algamish, you are a very rich man. Tell me how I may also become rich, and all night I will carve upon the clay, and when the sun rises it shall be completed.'

"He smiled at me and replied, 'You are a forward knave, but we will call it a bargain.'

"All that night I carved, though my back pained and the smell of the wick made my head ache until my eyes could hardly see. But when he returned at sunup the tablets were complete.

"'Now,' I said, 'tell me what you promised.'

"'You have fulfilled your part of our bargain, my son,' he said to me kindly, 'and I am ready to fulfil mine. I will tell you these things you wish to know because I am becoming an old man, and an old tongue loves to wag. And when youth comes to age for advise he receives the vision of years. But too often does youth think that age knows only the wisdom of the days that are gone, and therefore profits not. But remember this, the sun that shines today is the sun that shone when thy father was born, and will still be shining when thy last grandchild shall pass into the darkness.

"'The thoughts of youth,' he continued, 'are bright things that shine forth like the meteors that oft make brilliant the sky, but the wisdom of age is like the fixed stars that shine so unchanged that the sailor may depend upon them to steer his course.

"'Mark you well my words, for if you do not you will fail to grasp the truth that I will tell you, and you will think that your night's work has been in vain.'

"Then he looked at me shrewdly from under his shaggy brows and said in a low, forceful tone, 'I found the road to wealth when I decided that *a part of all I earned was mine to keep.* And so will you.'

"Then he continued to look at me with a glance that I could feel pierce me but said no more.

"'Is that all?' I asked.

"'That was sufficient to change the heart of a sheep herder into the heart of money lender,' he replied.

"'But all I earn is mine to keep, is it not?' I demanded.

"'Far from it,' he replied. 'Do you not pay the garment maker? Do you not pay the sandal maker? Do you not pay for the things you eat? Can you live in Babylon without spending? What have you to show for earnings of the past month? What for the past year? Fool! You pay to everyone but yourself. Dullard, you labor for others. As well be a slave and work for what your master gives you to eat and wear. If you did keep for yourself one-tenth of all you earn how much would you have in ten years?'

"My knowledge of the numbers did not forsake me, and I answered, 'As much as I earn in one year.'

"'You speak but half the truth,' he retorted. 'Every gold piece that you save is a slave to work for you. Every copper it earns is its child that also can earn for you. If you would become wealthy, then what you save must earn, and its children must earn, and its children's children must earn, that all may help to give to you the abundance you crave.

"'You think I cheat you for your long night's work,' he continued, 'but I am paying you a thousand times over if you have the intelligence to grasp the truth I offer you.

"'A PART OF ALL YOU EARN IS YOURS TO KEEP. It should not be less than a tenth no matter how little you earn. It can be as much more as you can afford. Pay yourself first. Do not buy from the clothes-maker and the sandal-maker more than you can pay out of the rest and still have enough for food and charity and penance to the gods.

"'Wealth, like a tree, grows from a tiny seed. The first copper you save is the seed from which your tree of wealth shall grow. The sooner you plant that seed the sooner shall the tree grow. And the more faithfully you nourish and water that tree with consistent savings, the sooner may you bask in contentment beneath its shade.' So saying, he took his tablets and went away.

"I thought much about what he had said to me, and it seemed reasonable. So I decided that I would try it. Each time I was paid I took one from each ten pieces of copper and hid it away. And strange as it may seem, I was no shorter of funds than before. I noticed little difference as I managed to get along without it. But often I was tempted as my hoard began to grow, to spend it for some of the good things the merchants displayed, brought by camels and ships from the land of the Phoenicians. But I wisely refrained.

"A twelve-month after Algamish had gone he again returned and said to me, 'Son, have you paid to yourself not less than one-tenth of all you have earned for the past year?'

"I answered proudly, 'Yes, master I have.'

"'That is good,' he answered, beaming upon me, 'And what have you done with it?'

"'I have given it to Azmur, the brick-maker, who told me he was travelling over the seven seas and in Tyre he would buy for me the rare jewels of the Phoenicians. When he returns we shall sell these at high prices and divide the earnings.'

"'Every fool must learn,' he growled, 'but why trust the knowledge of a brick-maker about jewels? Would you go to the bread-maker to inquire about the stars? No, by my tunic, you would go to the astrologer, if you had power to think. Your savings are gone, youth, you have jerked your wealth tree up by the roots. But plant another. Try again. And next time if you would have advice about jewels, go to the jewel merchant. If you would know the truth about sheep, go to the herdsman. Advice is one thing that is freely given away, but watch that you take only what is worth having. He who takes advice about his savings from one who is inexperienced in such matters, shall pay with his savings for proving the falsity of their opinions.' Saying this he went away.

"And it was as he said. For the Phoenicians are scoundrels and sold to Azmur worthless bits of glass that looked like gems. But as Algamish had bid me, I again saved each tenth copper, for I now had formed the habit and it was no longer difficult.

"A twelve-month later Algamish again came to the room of the scribes and addressed me. 'What progress have you made since last I saw you?'

"'I have paid myself faithfully,' I replied, 'and my savings I have entrusted to Aggar the shield-maker, to buy bronze, and each fourth month he does pay me the rental.'

"'That is good. And what do you do with the rental?'

"'I do have a great feast with honey and fine wine and spiced cake. Also I have bought me a scarlet tunic. And some day I shall buy me a young ass upon which to ride.'

"To which Algamish laughed. 'You do eat the children of your savings? Then how do you expect them to work for you? And how can they have children that will also work for you? First get thee an army of golden slaves and then many a rich banquet may you enjoy without regret.' So saying, he again went away.

"Nor did I again see him for two years, when he once more returned and his face was full of deep lines and his eyes drooped, for he was becoming a very old man. And he said to me, 'Arkad, hast thou yet achieved the wealth thou dreamed of?'

"And I answered, 'Not yet all that I desire, but some I have and it earns more, and its earnings earn more.'

"'And do you still take the advice of brick-makers?'

"'About brick-making they give good advice,' I retorted.

"'Arkad,' he continued, 'you have learned your lessons well. You first learned to live upon less than you could earn. Next you learned to seek advice from those who were competent through their own experience to give it. And lastly, you have learned to make gold work for you.

"'You have taught yourself how to acquire money, how to keep it, and how to use it. Therefore, you are competent for a responsible position. I am becoming an old man. My sons think only of spending and give no thought to earning. My interests are great and I fear too much for me to look after. If you will go to Nippur and look after my lands there, I shall make you my partner and you shall share in my estate.'

"'So I went to Nippur and took charge of his holdings, which were large. And because I was full of ambition and because I had mastered the three laws of successfully handling wealth, I was enabled to increase greatly the value of his properties. So I prospered much, and when the spirit of Algamish departed for the sphere of darkness, I did share in his estate as he had arranged under the law."

So spake Arkad, and when he had finished his tale, one of his friends said, "You were indeed fortunate that Algamish made of you an heir."

"Fortunate only in that I had the desire to prosper before I first met him. For four years did I not prove my definiteness of purpose by keeping one-tenth of all I earned? Would you call a fisherman lucky who for years so studied the habits of the fish that with each changing wind he could cast his nets about them? Opportunity is a haughty goddess who wastes no time with those who are unprepared."

"You had strong will power to keep on after you lost your first year's savings. You are unusual in that way," spoke up another.

"Will power!" retorted Arkad. "What nonsense. Do you think will power gives a man the strength to lift a burden the camel cannot carry, or to draw a load the oxen cannot budge? Will power is but the unflinching purpose to carry a task you set for yourself to fulfilment. If I set for myself a task, be it ever so trifling, I shall see it through. How else shall I have confidence in myself to do important things? Should I say to myself, 'For a hundred days as I walk across the bridge into the city, I will pick from the road a pebble and cast it into the stream,' I would do it. If on the seventh day I passed without remembering, I would not say to myself, 'Tomorrow I will cast two pebbles which will do as well.' Instead I would retrace my steps and cast the pebble. Nor on the twentieth day would I say to myself, 'Arkad, this is useless. What does it avail you to cast a pebble every day? Throw in a handful and be done with it.' No, I would not say that nor do it. When I set a task for myself, I complete it. Therefore am I careful not to start difficult and impractical tasks, because I love leisure."

And then another friend spoke up and said, "If what you tell us is true, and it does seem as you have said, reasonable, then being so simple, if all men did it, there would not be enough wealth to go around."

"Wealth grows wherever men exert energy," Arkad replied. "If a rich man builds him a new palace, is the gold he pays out gone? No, the brick-maker has part of it and the laborer has part of it, and the artist has part of it. And everyone who labors upon the house has part of it. Yet when the palace is completed, is it not worth all it cost? And is the ground upon which it stands not worth more because it is there? And is the ground that adjoins it not worth more because it is there? Wealth grows in magic ways. No man can prophesy the limit of it. Have not the Phoenicians built great cities on barren coasts with the wealth that comes from their ships of commerce on the seas?

"What, then, do you advise us to do that we also may become rich?" asked still another of his friends. "The years have passed and we are no longer young men and we have nothing put by."

"I advise that you take the wisdom of Algamish and say to yourselves, 'A part of all I earn is mine to keep.' Say it in the morning when you first arise. Say it at noon. Say it at night. Say it each hour of every day. Say it to yourself until the words stand out like letters of fire across the sky.

"Impress yourself with the idea. Fill your self with the thought. Then take whatever portion seems wise. Let it be not less than one-tenth and lay it by. Arrange your other expenditures to do this if necessary. But lay by that portion first. Soon you will realize what a rich feeling it is to have something upon which you alone have claim. As it grows it will stimulate you. A new joy of life will thrill you. Greater efforts will come to you to earn more. For of your increased earnings, will not the same percentage be also yours to keep?

"Then learn to make your treasure work for you. Make it your slave. Make its children and its children's children work for you.

"Insure an income for thy future. Look thou at the aged and forget not that in the days to come thou also will be numbered among them. Therefore invest thy treasures with greatest caution that it be not lost. Usurious rates of return are deceitful sirens that sing but to lure the unwary upon the rocks of loss and remorse.

"Provide also that thy family may not want should the gods call thee to their realms. For such protection, it is always possible to make provision with small payments at regular intervals. Therefore the provident man delays not in expectation of a large sum becoming available for such a wise purpose.

"Counsel with wise men. Seek the advice of men whose daily work is handling money. Let them save you from such an error as I myself made in entrusting my money to the judgment of Azmur, the brick-maker. A small return and a safe one is far more desirable than risk.

"Enjoy life while you are here. Do not over strain or try to save too much. If one-tenth of all you earn is as much as you can comfortably keep, be content to keep this portion. Live otherwise according to your income and let not yourself get niggardly and afraid to spend. Life is good and life is rich with things worth while and things to enjoy."

His friends thanked him and went away. Some were silent because they had no imagination and could not understand. Some were sarcastic because they thought that one so rich should divide with old friends not so fortunate. But some had in their eyes a new light. They realized that Algamish had come back each time to the room of the scribes because he was watching a man work his way out of darkness into light. When that man had found the light, a place awaited him. No one could fill that place until he had for himself worked out his own understanding, until he was ready for opportunity.

These latter were the ones, who, in the following years frequently revisited Arkad, who received them gladly. He counselled with them and gave them freely of his wisdom as men of broad experience are always glad to do. And he assisted them in so investing their savings that it would bring in a good interest with safety and would neither be lost nor entangled in investments that paid no dividends.

THE TURNING POINT in these men's lives came upon that day when they realized the truth that had come from Algamish to Arkad and from Arkad to them.

A PART OF ALL YOU EARN IS YOURS TO KEEP

Out of the Ruins
— of —
Babylon

A Tale of Conquest

A message for every man and woman who has ambitions to accomplish and ideals to uphold, a message so important that after five thousand years, it has risen out of the ruins of Babylon, just as true and just as vital as the day it was buried.

The Tale of the Clay Tablets from Babylon

Foreword

Clay Tablets is a name applied to the written records of ancient Babylon. Instead of using paper, which they did not have, they engraved their writings upon blocks of moist clay and burned these to make them permanent. These Tablets were about an inch in thickness and slightly larger than a modern house brick.

The Babylonians were prolific writers. Hundreds of thousands of their clay tablets have been recovered by modern scientific expeditions and are being deciphered by trained archaeologists. Many of these records refer to the sale of property and give details of business transactions. Others are messages or letters as we would consider them. Still another class give the laws of the land as proclaimed by the wise king, Hammurabi, laws just as fair and equitable as any we have today.

In the homes and marts of trades the tablets were usually stored in large earthen jars. In the royal libraries of the kings, they were arranged upon shelves similar to books in a modern library. Lengthy documents would require many of these bulky tablets. A single tablet would contain less writing than a page of a modern book, therefore much storage space was required. Where many tablets were required for single documents, these were carefully indexed by means of tabs hanging from straws.

We are indeed fortunate that the records of the ancient Babylonian civilization were in so permanent a form. Otherwise they would have been lost forever.

The eons of time have crumbled to dust the proud walls of its temples, but the wisdom of Babylon endures and to this wisdom we may look for wise solutions to many of the perplexing problems which confront us as individuals, today.

Out of the Ruins of Babylon

ST. SWITHIN'S COLLEGE

NOTTINGHAM UNIVERSITY
NEWARK-ON-TRENT
NOTTINGHAM

October 21, 1930

Professor Franklin Caldwell,
Care of British Scientific Expedition,
Hillah, Mesopotamia.

My dear Professor:

The five clay tablets from your recent excavation in the ruins of Babylon arrived on the same boat with your letter. I have been fascinated to no end, and have spent many pleasant hours translating their inscriptions. I should have answered your letter at once but delayed until I could complete the translations, which are attached.

The tablets arrived without damage, thanks to your careful use of preservatives and excellent packing.

You will be as astonished as we in the laboratory, at the story they relate. One expects the dim and distant past to speak of romance and adventure. "Arabian Nights" sort of things, you know. When instead it discloses the problem of a person named Dabasir, to pay off his debts, one realizes that conditions upon this old world have not changed as much in five thousand years as one might expect.

It's odd, you know, but these old inscriptions rather 'rag' me, as the students say. Being a college professor, I am supposed to be a thinking human being possessing a working knowledge upon most subjects. Yet, here comes this old chap out of the dust-covered ruins of Babylon to offer a way I had never heard of to pay off my debts and at the same time acquire gold to jingle in my wallet.

Pleasant thought, I say, and interesting to prove whether it will work as well nowadays as it did in old Babylon. Mrs. Shrewsbury and myself are planning to try out his plan upon our own affairs which could be much improved.

Wishing you the best of luck in your worthy undertaking and awaiting eagerly another opportunity to assist, I am,

Yours sincerely,

Alfred H. Shrewsbury,

Department of Archaeology.

TABLET No. I

Now when the moon becometh full I, Dabasir, who am but recently returned from slavery in Syria, with the determination to pay my many just debts and become a man of means worthy of respect in my native city of Babylon, do here engrave upon the clay a permanent record of my affairs to guide and assist me in carrying through my high desires.

Under the wise advice of my good friend Mathon, the gold lender, I am determined to follow an exact plan that he doth say will lead any honorable man out of debt into means and self-respect.

This plan includeth three purposes which are my hope and desire.

First, the PLAN doth provide for my future prosperity.

Therefore one-tenth of all I earn shall be set aside as my own to keep. For Mathon speaketh wisely when he saith:

"That man who keepeth in his purse both gold and silver that he need not spend is good to his family and loyal to his king.

"The man who hath but a few coppers in his purse, is indifferent to his family and indifferent to his king.

"But the man who hath naught in his purse, is unkind to his family and is disloyal to his king for his own heart is bitter.

"Therefore, the man who wisheth to achieve must have coin that he may keep to jingle in his purse, that he have in his heart love for his family and loyalty to his king."

Second, the PLAN doth provide that I shall support and clothe my good wife who hath returned to me with loyalty from the house of her father. For Mathon doth say that to take good care of a faithful wife putteth self-respect into the heart of a man and addeth strength and determination to his purposes.

Therefore seven-tenths of all I earn shall be used to provide a home, clothes to wear, and food to eat, with a bit extra to spend, that our lives be not lacking in pleasure and enjoyment. But he doth further enjoin the greatest care that we spend not greater than seven-tenths of what I earn for these worthy purposes. Herein lieth the success of the PLAN. I must live upon this portion and never use more nor buy what I may not pay for out of this portion.

TABLET No. II

Third, the PLAN doth provide that out of my earnings my debts shall be paid.

Therefore each time the moon is full, two-tenths of all I have earned shall be divided honorably and fairly among those who have trusted me and to whom I am indebted. Thus in due time will all my indebtedness be surely paid.

Therefore, do I here engrave the names of every man to whom I am indebted and the honest amount of my debt.

Fahru, the cloth weaver, 2 silver, 6 copper.

Sinjar, the couch maker, 1 silver.

Ahmar, my friend, 3 silver, 1 copper.

Zankar, my friend, 4 silver, 7 copper.

Askanir, my friend, 1 silver, 3 copper.

Harinsir, the jewelmaker, 6 silver, 2 copper.

Diarbeker, my father's friend, 4 silver, 1 copper.

Alkahad, the house owner, 14 silver.

Mathon, the gold lender, 9 silver.

Birejik, the farmer, 1 silver, 7 copper.

(From here on, disintegrated. Cannot be deciphered.)

TABLET No. III

To these creditors do I owe in total one hundred and nineteen pieces of silver and one hundred and forty-one pieces of copper. Because I did owe these sums and saw no way to repay, in my folly I didst permit my wife to return to her father and didst leave my native city and seek easy wealth elsewhere, only to find disaster and to see myself sold into the degradation of slavery.

Now that Mathon doth show me how I can repay my debts in small sums out of my earnings, do I realize the great extent of my folly in running away from the results of my extravagances.

Therefore I have visited my creditors and explained to them that I have no resources with which to pay except my ability to earn, and that I intend to apply two-tenths of all I earn upon my indebtedness, evenly and honestly. This much can I pay but no more. Therefore if they be patient, in time my obligations will be paid in full.

Ahmar, whom I thought my best friend, reviled me bitterly and I left him in humiliation. Birejik, the farmer, pleaded that I pay him first as he didst badly need help. Alkahad, the house owner, was indeed disagreeable and insisted that he would make me trouble unless I didst soon settle in full with him.

All the rest willingly accepted my proposal. Therefore am I more determined than ever to carry through, being convinced that it is easier to pay one's just debts than to avoid them. Even though I cannot meet the needs and demands of a few of my creditors I will deal impartially with all.

TABLET No. IV

Again the moon shines full. I have worked hard with a free mind. My good wife hath supported my intentions to pay my creditors.

Because of our wise determination, I have earned during the past moon, buying camels of sound wind and good legs, for Nebatur, the sum of nineteen pieces of silver.

This I have divided according to the PLAN. One-tenth have I set aside to keep as my own, seven-tenths have I divided with my good wife to pay for our living. Two-tenths have I divided among my creditors as evenly as could be done in coppers.

I did not see Ahmar but left it with his wife. Birejik was so pleased he would kiss my hand. Old Alkahad alone was grouchy and said I must pay faster. To which I replied that if I were permitted to be well fed and not worried, that alone would enable me to pay faster. All the others thanked me and spoke well of my efforts.

Therefore, at the end of one moon, my indebtedness is reduced by almost four pieces of silver and I possess almost two pieces of silver besides, upon which no man hath claim. My heart is lighter than it hath been for a long time.

Again the moon shines full. I have worked hard but with poor success. Few camels have I been able to buy. Only eleven pieces of silver have I earned. Nevertheless my good wife and I have stood by the plan even though we have bought no new raiment and eaten little but herbs. Again I paid ourselves one-tenth of the eleven pieces, while we lived upon seven-tenths. I was surprised when Ahmar commended my payment, even though small. So did Birejik. Alkahad flew into a rage but when told to give back his portion if he did not wish it, he became reconciled. The others as before were content.

Again the moon shines full and I am greatly rejoiced. I intercepted a fine herd of camels and bought many sound ones, therefore my earnings were forty-two pieces of silver. This moon my wife and myself have bought much needed sandals and raiment. Also we have dined well on meat and fowl.

More than eight pieces of silver we have paid to our creditors. Even Alkahad did not protest.

Great is the PLAN for it leadeth us out of debt and giveth us wealth which is ours to keep.

Three times the moon hath been full since I last carved upon this clay. Each time I paid to myself one-tenth of all I earned. Each time my good wife and I have lived upon seven-tenths even though at times it was difficult. Each time have I paid to my creditors two-tenths.

In my purse I now have twenty-one pieces of silver that is mine; more than I ever owned at one time before. It maketh my head to stand straight upon my shoulders and maketh me proud to walk among my friends.

My wife keepeth well our home and is becomingly gowned. We are happy to live together.

The PLAN is of untold value. Hath it not made an honorable man of an ex-slave.

TABLET No. V

Again the moon shines full and I remember that it is long since I carved upon the clay. Twelve moons in truth have come and gone. But this day I will not neglect my record because upon this day I have paid the last of my debts. This is the day upon which my good wife and my thankful self celebrate with great feasting that our determination hath been achieved.

Many things occurred upon my final visit to my creditors that I shall long remember. Ahmar begged my forgiveness for his unkind words and said that I was one of all others he most desired for a friend.

Old Alkahad is not so bad after all, for he said, "Thou wert once a piece of soft clay to be pressed and moulded by any hand that touched thee, but now thou are a piece of bronze capable of holding an edge. If thou needst silver or gold at any time come to me."

Nor is he the only one who holdeth me in high regard. Many others speak deferentially to me. My good wife looketh upon me with a light in her eyes that doth make a man have confidence in himself.

Yet it is the PLAN that hath made my success. It hath enabled me to pay all my debts and to jingle both gold and silver in my purse. I do commend it to all who wish to get ahead. For truly if it will enable an ex-slave to pay his debts and have gold in his purse, will it not aid any man to find independence? Nor am I, myself, finished with it, for I am convinced that if I follow it further it will make me rich among men.

ST. SWITHIN'S COLLEGE

NOTTINGHAM UNIVERSITY
NEWARK-ON-TRENT
NOTTINGHAM

November 7th, 1932.

Professor Franklin Caldwell,
Care of British Scientific Expedition,
Hillah, Mesopotamia.

My dear professor:

If, in your further digging into those bally ruins of Babylon, you encounter the ghost of a former resident, an old camel trader named Dabasir, do me a favor. Tell him that his scribbling upon those clay tablets, so long ago, has earned for him the life-long gratitude of a couple of college folks back here in England.

You will possibly remember my writing a year ago that Mrs. Shrewsbury and myself intended to try his plan for getting out of debt and at the same time having gold to jingle. You may have guessed, even though we tried to keep from our friends, our desperate straits.

We were frightfully humiliated for years by a lot of old debts and worried sick for fear some of the

47

tradespeople might start a scandal that would force me out of the college. We paid and paid—every shilling we could squeeze out of income, but it was hardly enough to hold things even. Besides we were forced to do all our buying where we could get further credit regardless of higher costs.

It developed into one of those vicious circles that grow worse instead of better. Our struggles were getting hopeless. We could not move to less costly rooms because we owed the landlord. There did not appear to be anything we could do to improve our situation.

Then, here comes your acquaintance, the old camel trader from Babylon, with a plan to do just what we wished to accomplish. He jolly well stirred us up to follow his system. We made a list of all our debts and I took it around and showed it to every one we owed.

I explained how it was simply impossible for me to ever pay them the way things were going along. They could readily see this themselves from the figures. Then I explained that the only way I saw to pay in full was to set aside twenty per cent of my income each month to be divided *pro rata*, which would pay them in full in a little over two years. That, in the meantime, we would go on a cash basis and give them the further benefit of our cash purchases.

They were really quite decent. Our greengrocer, a wise old chap, put it in a way that helped to bring around the rest. "If you pay for all you buy and then pay some on what you owe, that is better than you have done, for ye ain't paid down the account none in three years."

Finally I secured all their names to an agreement binding them not to molest us as long as the twenty per cent of income was paid regularly. Then we began scheming on how to live upon seventy per cent. We were determined to keep that extra ten per cent to jingle. The thought of silver and possibly gold was most alluring.

It was like having an adventure to make the change. We enjoyed figuring this way and that, to live comfortably upon that remaining seventy per cent. Started with rent and managed to secure a fair reduction. Next we put our favorite brands of tea and such under suspicion and were agreeably surprised how often we could purchase superior qualities at less cost.

It is too long a story for a letter but anyhow it did not prove difficult. We managed and right cheerfully at that. What a relief it proved to have our affairs in such a shape we were no longer persecuted by past due accounts.

I must not neglect, however, to tell you about that extra ten per cent we were supposed to jingle. Well, we did jingle it for some time. Now don't laugh too soon. You see, that is the sporty part. It is the real fun, to start accumulating money that you do not want to spend. There is more pleasure in running up such a surplus than there could be in spending it.

After we had jingled to our hearts content, we found a more profitable use for it. We took up an investment upon which we could pay that ten per cent each month. This is proving to be the most satisfying part of our regeneration. It is the first thing we pay out of my cheque.

There is a most gratifying sense of security to know our investment is growing steadily. By the time my teaching days are over it should be a snug sum, large enough so the income will take care of us from then on.

All this out of my same old cheque. Difficult to believe, yet absolutely true. All our old debts being gradually paid and at the same time our investment increasing. Besides we get along, financially, even better than before. Who would believe there could be such a difference in results between following a financial plan and just drifting along.

At the end of the next year, when all our old bills shall have been paid, we will have more to pay upon our investment besides some extra for travel. We are determined never again to permit our living expenses to exceed seventy per cent of our income.

Now you can understand why we would like to extend our personal thanks to that old chap whose plan saved us from our 'Hell on Earth,' DEBTS.

He knew. He had been through it all. He wanted others to benefit from his own bitter experiences. That is why he spent tedious hours carving his message upon the clay.

He had a real message for fellow sufferers, a message so important that after five thousand years it has risen out of the Ruins of Babylon, just as true and just as vital as the day it was buried.

Yours sincerely,

Alfred H. Shrewsbury,

Department of Archaeology.

Seven Remedies
—— for a ——
Lean Purse

A Tale of Babylon

The Tale of Seven Remedies for A Lean Purse

A Tale of Babylon

THE glory of Babylon endures. Down through the ages its reputation comes to us as the richest of cities, its treasures as fabulous.

Yet it was not always so. The riches of Babylon were the results of the money wisdom of its people. They first had to learn how to become wealthy.

About the year 3800 B.C., when the good king, SARGON I, returned to Babylon after defeating his enemies, the Elamites, he was confronted with a serious situation. The royal Chancellor explained it to the king thus:

"After many years of great prosperity brought to our people because your majesty built the great irrigation canals and the mighty temples to the gods, now that these works are completed the people seem unable to support themselves.

"The laborers are without employment. The merchants have few customers. The farmers are unable to sell their produce. The people have not enough gold to buy food."

"But where has all the gold gone that we spent for these great improvements?" demanded the king.

"It has found its way, I fear," responded the Chancellor, "into the possession of a few very rich men of our city. It filtered through the fingers of most of our people as quickly as the goat's milk goes through the strainer. Now that the stream of gold has ceased to flow, most of our people have nothing to show for their earnings."

The king was thoughtful for some time. Then he asked, "Why should so few men be able to acquire all the gold?"

"Because they know how," replied the Chancellor. "One may not condemn a man for succeeding because he knows how. Neither may one with justice take away from a man what he has fairly earned, to give to men of less ability."

"But why," demanded the king, "should not all the people learn how to accumulate gold and therefore become themselves rich and prosperous?"

"Quite possible, your excellency. But who can teach them? Certainly not the priests, because they know naught of money making."

"Who knows best in all our city how to become wealthy, Chancellor?" asked the king.

"Thy question answers itself, your majesty. Who has amassed the greatest wealth in Babylon?"

"Well said, my able Chancellor. It is Arkad. He is the richest man in Babylon. Bring him before me on the morrow."

Upon the following day, as the king had decreed, Arkad appeared before him, straight and sprightly despite his three score years and ten.

"Arkad," spoke the king, "is it true thou art the richest man in Babylon?"

"So it is reported, your majesty, and no man disputes it."

"How becamest thou so wealthy?"

"By taking advantage of opportunities available to all citizens of our good city."

"Thou hadst nothing to start with?"

"Only a great desire for wealth. Besides this, nothing."

"Arkad," continued the king, "our city is in a very unhappy state because a few men know how to acquire wealth and therefore monopolize it, while the mass of our citizens lack the knowledge of how to keep any part of the gold they receive.

"It is my desire that Babylon be the wealthiest city in the world. Therefore, it must be a city of many wealthy men. Therefore, we must teach all the people how to acquire riches. Tell me, Arkad, is there any secret to acquiring wealth? Can it be taught?"

"It is practical, your majesty. That which one man knows can be taught to others."

The king's eyes glowed. "Arkad, thou speaketh the words I wish to hear. Wilt thou lend thyself to this great cause? Wilt thou teach thy knowledge to a school for teachers, each of whom shall teach others until there are enough trained to teach these truths to every worthy subject in my domain?"

Arkad bowed and said, "I am thy humble servant to command. Whatever of knowledge I possess will I gladly give for the betterment of my fellow men and the glory of my king. Let your good chancellor arrange for me a class of one hundred men and I will teach to them those Seven Remedies which did fatten my purse, than which there was none leaner in all Babylon."

A fortnight later, in compliance with the king's command, the chosen hundred assembled in the great hall of the Temple of Learning, seated upon colorful rugs in a semi-circle. Arkad sat beside a small taboret upon which smoked a sacred lamp sending forth a strange and pleasing odor.

"Behold the richest man in Babylon," whispered a student, nudging his neighbor as Arkad arose. "He is but a man even as the rest of us."

"As a dutiful subject of our great king," Arkad began. "I stand before you in his service. Because once I was a poor youth who did greatly desire gold, and because I found knowledge that enabled me to acquire it, he asks that I impart unto you my knowledge.

"I started my fortune in the humblest way. I had no advantage not enjoyed as fully by you and every citizen of Babylon.

"The first storehouse of my treasure was a well-worn purse. I loathed its useless emptiness. I desired that it be round and full, clinking with the sound of gold. Therefore, I sought every remedy for a lean purse. I found seven.

"To you who are assembled before me, shall I explain the 'Seven Remedies for a Lean Purse' which I do recommend to all men who desire much gold. Each day for seven days will I explain to you one of the Seven Remedies.

"Listen attentively to the knowledge that I will impart. Debate it with me. Discuss it among yourselves. Learn these lessons thoroughly, that ye may also plant in your own purses the seed of wealth. First must each of you start wisely to build a fortune of his own. Then wilt thou be competent, and only then, to teach these truths to others.

"I shall teach to you in simple ways how to fatten your purses. This is the first step leading to the temple of wealth, and no man may climb who cannot plant his feet firmly upon the first step.

"We shall now consider the First Remedy."

THE FIRST REMEDY
Start Thy Purse To Fattening

Arkad addressed a thoughtful man in the second row. "My good friend, at what craft workest thou?"

"I," replied the man, "am a scribe and carve records upon the clay tablets."

"Even at such labor did I myself earn my first coppers. Therefore, thou hast the same opportunity to build a fortune."

He spoke to a florid-faced man, farther back.

"Pray tell also what dost thou to earn thy bread."

"I," responded this man, "am a meat butcher. I do buy the goats the farmers raise and kill them and sell the meat to the housewives and the hides to the sandal makers."

"Because thou dost also labor and earn, thou hast every advantage to succeed that I did possess."

In this way did Arkad proceed to find out how each man labored to earn his living. When he had done questioning them, he said:

"Now, my students, ye can see that there are many trades and labors at which men may earn coins. Each of the ways of earning is a stream of gold from which the worker doth divert by his labors a portion to his own purse. Therefore into the purse of each of you flows a stream of coins large or small according to his ability. Is it not so?"

Thereupon they agreed that it was so.

"Then," continued Arkad, "if each of you desireth to build for himself a fortune, is it not wise to start by utilizing that source of wealth which he already has established?"

To this they agreed.

Then Arkad turned to a humble man who had declared himself an egg merchant. "If thou select one of thy baskets and put into it each morning ten eggs and take out from it each evening nine eggs, what will eventually happen?"

"It will become in time overflowing."

"Why?"

"Because each day I put in one more egg than I take out."

Arkad turned to his class with a smile. "Does any man here have a lean purse?"

First they looked amused. Then they laughed. Lastly they waved their purses in jest.

"All right," he continued, "now I shall tell thee the first remedy I learned to cure a lean purse. Do exactly as I have suggested to the egg merchant. FOR EVERY TEN COINS THOU PLACEST WITHIN THY PURSE TAKE OUT FOR USE BUT NINE. THY PURSE WILL START TO FATTEN AT ONCE AND ITS INCREASING WEIGHT WILL FEEL GOOD IN THY HAND AND BRING SATISFACTION TO THY SOUL.

"Deride not what I say because of its simplicity. Truth is always simple. I told thee I would tell how I built my fortune. This was my beginning. I, too, carried a lean purse and cursed it because there was naught within to satisfy my desires. But when

I began to take out from my purse but nine part ten I put in, it began to fatten. So will thine.

"Now I will tell a strange truth, the reason for which I know not, when I ceased to pay out more than nine-tenths of my earnings, I managed to get along just as well. I was not shorter than before. Also, ere long, did coins come to me more easily than before. Surely it is a law of the gods that unto him who keepeth and spendeth not a certain part of all his earning, shall gold come more easily. Likewise, him whose purse is empty does gold avoid.

"Which desirest thou the most? Is it the gratification of thy desires of each day, a jewel, a bit of finery, better raiment, more food; things quickly gone and forgotten? Or is it substantial belongings, gold, lands, herds, merchandise, income bringing investments? The coins thou takest from thy purse bring the first. The coins thou leavest within it will bring the latter.

"THIS, MY STUDENTS. WAS THE FIRST REMEDY I DID DISCOVER FOR MY LEAN PURSE: 'FOR EACH TEN COINS I PUT IN, TO SPEND BUT NINE.' Debate this amongst yourselves. If any man proves it untrue tell me upon the morrow when we shall meet again."

THE SECOND REMEDY
Control Thy Expenditures

"Some of your members, my students, have asked me this: 'How can a man keep one-tenth of all he earns in his purse when all the coins he earns are not enough for his necessary expenses?'" So did Arkad address his students upon the second day.

"Yesterday how many of you carried lean purses?"

"All of us," answered the class.

"Yet, thou do not all earn the same. Some earn much more than others. Some have much larger families to support. Yet, all purses were equally lean. Now I will tell thee an unusual truth about men and sons of men. It is this: That which each of us calls our necessary expenses will always grow to equal our incomes unless we protest to the contrary.

"CONFUSE NOT THY NECESSARY EXPENSES WITH THY DESIRES. EACH OF YOU, TOGETHER WITH YOUR GOOD FAMILIES, HAVE MORE DESIRES THAN YOUR EARNINGS CAN GRATIFY. Therefore, are thy earnings spent to gratify these desires in so far as they will go. Still thou retainest many ungratified desires.

"All men are burdened with more desires than they can gratify. Because of my wealth thinkest thou I may gratify every desire? 'Tis a false idea. There are limits to my time. There are limits to my strength. There are limits to the distance I may travel. There are limits to what I may eat. There are limits to the zest with which I may enjoy.

"I say to you that just as weeds grow in a field wherever the farmer leaves space for their roots, even so freely do desires grow in men whenever there is a possibilty of their being gratified. THY DESIRES ARE A MULTITUDE AND THOSE THAT THOU MAYEST GRATIFY ARE BUT FEW.

"Study thoughtfully thy accustomed habits of living. Herein may be most often found certain accepted expenses that may wisely be reduced or eliminated. Let thy motto be one hundred per cent of appreciated value demanded for each coin spent.

"THEREFORE, ENGRAVE UPON THE CLAY EACH THING FOR WHICH THOU DESIREST TO SPEND. SELECT THOSE THAT ARE NECESSARY AND OTHERS THAT ARE POSSIBLE THROUGH THE EXPENDITURE OF NINE-TENTHS OF THY INCOME. CROSS OUT THE REST AND CONSIDER THEM BUT

A PART OF THAT GREAT MULTITUDE OF DESIRES THAT MUST GO UNSATISFIED AND REGRET THEM NOT.

"Budget then thy necessary expenses. Touch not the one-tenth that is fattening thy purse. Let this be thy great desire that is being fulfilled. Keep working with thy budget, keep adjusting it to help thee. Make it thy first assistant in defending thy fattening purse."

Hereupon one of the students, wearing a robe of red and gold, arose and said, "I am a free man. I believe that it is my right to enjoy the good things of life. Therefore do I rebel against the slavery of a budget which determines just how much I may spend and for what. I feel it would take much pleasure from my life and make me little more than a pack-ass to carry a burden."

To him Arkad replied. "Who, my friend, would determine thy budget?"

"I would make it for myself," responded the protesting one.

"In that case were a pack-ass to budget his burden would he include therein jewels and rugs and heavy bars of gold? Not so. He would include hay and grain and a bag of water for the desert trail.

"The purpose of a budget is to help thy purse to fatten. It is to assist thee to have thy necessities and, in so far as attainable, thy other desires. It is to enable thee to realize thy most cherished desires by defending them from thy casual wishes. Like a bright light in a dark cave thy budget shows up the leaks from thy purse and enables thee to stop them and control thy expenditures for definite and gratifying purposes.

"THIS, THEN, IS THE SECOND REMEDY FOR A LEAN PURSE. BUDGET THY EXPENSES THAT THOU MAYEST HAVE COINS TO PAY FOR THY NECESSITIES, TO PAY FOR THY ENJOYMENTS AND TO GRATIFY THY WORTHWHILE DESIRES WITHOUT SPENDING MORE THAN NINE-TENTHS OF THY EARNINGS."

THE THIRD REMEDY
Make Thy Gold Multiply

"Behold thy lean purse is fattening. Thou hast disciplined thyself to leave therein one-tenth of all thou earneth. Thou hast controlled thy expenditures to protect thy growing treasure. Next, we will consider means to put thy treasure to labor and to increase. GOLD IN A PURSE IS GRATIFYING TO OWN AND SATISFIETH A MISERLY SOUL BUT EARNS NOTHING. THE GOLD WE MAY RETAIN FROM OUR EARNINGS IS BUT THE START. THE EARNINGS IT WILL MAKE SHALL BUILD OUR FORTUNES." So spoke Arkad upon the third day to his class.

"How, therefore, may we put our gold to work? My first investment was unfortunate, for I lost all. Its tale I will relate later. My first profitable investment was a loan to a man named Aggar, a shield-maker. Once each year did he buy large shipments of bronze brought from across the sea to use in his trade. Lacking sufficient capital to pay the merchants, he would borrow from those who had extra coins. He was an honorable man. His borrowing he would repay, together with a liberal rental, as he sold his shields.

"Each time I loaned to him I loaned back also the rental he had paid me. Therefore not only did my capital increase, but its earning likewise increased. Most gratifying was it to have these sums return to my purse.

"I tell you, my students, a man's wealth is not in the coins he carries in his purse; it is the income he buildeth, the golden stream that continually floweth into his purse and keepeth it always bulging. That is what every man desireth. That is what thou, each one of thee, desireth; an income that continueth to come whether thou work or travel.

"Great income I have acquired. So great that I am called a very rich man. My loans to Aggar were my first training in profitable investment. Gaining wisdom from this experience, I extended my loans and investments as my capital increased. From a few sources at first, from many sources later, flowed into my purse a golden stream of wealth available for such wise uses as I should decide.

"BEHOLD, FROM MY HUMBLE EARNINGS I HAD BEGOTTEN A HOARD OF GOLDEN SLAVES, EACH LABORING AND EARNING MORE GOLD. AS THEY LABORED FOR ME, SO THEIR CHILDREN ALSO LABORED AND THEIR CHILDREN'S CHILDREN UNTIL GREAT WAS THE INCOME FROM THEIR COMBINED EFFORTS.

"Gold increaseth rapidly when making reasonable earnings as thou wilt see from the following: A farmer when his first son was born, took ten pieces of silver to a money lender and asked him to keep it on rental for his son until he became twenty years of age. This the money lender did, and agreed the rental should be one-fourth of its value each four years. The farmer asked, because this sum he had set aside as belonging to his son, that the rental be added to the principal.

"When the boy had reached the age of twenty years, the farmer again went to the money lender to inquire about the silver. The money lender explained that because this sum had been increased by compound interest, the original ten pieces of silver had now grown to thirty and one-half pieces.

"The farmer was well pleased and because the son did not need the coins, he left them with the money lender. When the son became fifty years of age, the father meantime having passed to the other world, the money lender paid the son in settlement one hundred and sixty-seven pieces of silver.

"Thus in fifty years had the investment multiplied itself at rental almost seventeen times.

"THIS, THEN IS THE THIRD REMEDY FOR A LEAN PURSE, TO PUT EACH COIN TO LABORING THAT IT MAY REPRODUCE ITS KIND EVEN AS THE FLOCKS OF THE FIELD AND HELP BRING TO THEE INCOME,

A STREAM OF WEALTH THAT SHALL FLOW CONSTANTLY INTO THY PURSE."

THE FOURTH REMEDY
Guard Thy Treasures From Loss

"Misfortune loves a shining mark. Gold in a man's purse must be guarded with firmness, else it be lost. Thus it is wise that we must first secure small amounts and learn to protect them before the gods entrust us with larger." So spoke Arkad upon the fourth day to his class.

"Every owner of gold is tempted by opportunities whereby it would seem that he could make larger sums by its investment in most plausible projects. Often friends and relatives are eagerly entering such investments and urge him to follow.

"THE FIRST SOUND PRINCIPLE OF INVESTMENT IS SECURITY FOR THY PRINCIPAL. IS IT WISE TO BE INTRIGUED BY LARGER EARNINGS WHEN THY PRINCIPAL MAY BE LOST? I SAY NOT. THE PENALTY OF RISK IS PROBABLE LOSS. STUDY CAREFULLY BEFORE PARTING WITH THY TREASURE EACH ASSURANCE, THAT IT MAY BE SAFELY RECLAIMED. BE NOT MISLED BY THY OWN

ROMANTIC DESIRES TO MAKE WEALTH RAPIDLY.

"Before thou loan it to any man assure thyself of his ability to repay and his reputation for doing so, that thou mayest not unwittingly be making him a present of thy hard-earned treasure.

"Before thou entrust it as an investment in any field acquaint thyself with the dangers which may beset it.

"My own first investment was a tragedy to me at the time. The guarded savings of a year I did entrust to a brick-maker, named Azmur, who was travelling over the far seas and in Tyre agreed to buy for me the rare jewels of the Phoenicians. These we would sell upon his return and divide the profits. The Phoenicians were scoundrels and sold him bits of glass. My treasure was lost. Today, my training would show to me at once the folly of entrusting a brick-maker to buy jewels.

"THEREFORE, DO I ADVISE THEE FROM THE WISDOM OF MY EXPERIENCES: BE NOT TOO CONFIDENT OF THY OWN WISDOM IN ENTRUSTING THY TREASURES TO THE POSSIBLE PITFALLS OF INVESTMENTS. Better far to consult the wisdom of those experienced in handling money for profit. Such advice is freely given for the asking and may readily possess a value equal in gold to the sum thou considerest investing. In truth such is its actual value, if it save thee from loss.

"This, then, is the fourth remedy for a lean purse, and of great importance if it prevent thy purse from being emptied once it has become well-filled. GUARD THY TREASURE FROM LOSS BY INVESTING ONLY WHERE THY PRINCIPAL IS SAFE, WHERE IT MAY BE RECLAIMED IF DESIRABLE, AND WHERE THOU WILL NOT FAIL TO COLLECT A FAIR RENTAL. CONSULT WITH WISE MEN. SECURE THE ADVICE OF MEN EXPERIENCED IN THE PROFITABLE HANDLING OF GOLD. LET THEIR WISDOM PROTECT THY TREASURE FROM UNSAFE INVESTMENT."

THE FIFTH REMEDY
Make of Thy Dwelling a Profitable Investment

"If a man setteth aside nine parts of his earnings upon which to live and enjoy life, and if any part of this nine parts can he turn into a profitable investment without detriment to his well being, then so much faster will his treasures grow." So spake Arkad to his class at their fifth lesson.

"All too many of our men of Babylon do raise their families in unseemly quarters. They do pay to exacting landlords liberal rentals for rooms where their wives have not a spot to raise the blooms that gladden a woman's heart and their children have no place to play their games except in the unclean alleys.

"No man's family can fully enjoy life unless they do have a plot of ground wherein children can play in the clean earth and where the wife may raise not only blossoms, but good rich herbs to feed her family.

"To a man's heart it brings gladness to eat the figs from his own trees and the grapes of his own vines. To own his own domicile and to have it a place he is proud to care for putteth confidence in his heart and greater effort behind all his endeavors. Therefore, do I recommend that every man own the roof that sheltereth him and his.

"Nor is it beyond the ability of any well-intentioned man to own his home. Hath not our great king so widely extended the walls of Babylon that within them much land is now unused and may be purchased at sums most reasonable?

"Also I say to you, my students, that the money lenders gladly consider the desires of men who seek homes and lands for their families. Readily may thou borrow to pay the brickmaker and the builder for such commendable purposes, if thou can show a reasonable portion of the necessary sum which thou thyself hath provided for the purpose. "Then when the house be built, thou canst pay the money lender with the same regularity as thou didst pay the landlord. Because each payment will reduce thy indebtedness to the money lender, a few years will satisfy his loan.

"Then will thy heart be glad because thou wilt own in thy own right a valuable property and thy only cost will be the king's taxes.

"Also wilt thy good wife go more often to the river to wash thy robes, that each time returning she may bring a goatskin of water to pour upon the growing things.

"THUS COMES MANY BLESSINGS TO THE MAN WHO OWNETH HIS OWN HOUSE. AND GREATLY WILL IT REDUCE HIS COST OF LIVING, MAKING AVAILABLE MORE OF HIS EARNINGS FOR PLEASURES AND THE GRAT-IFICATION OF HIS DESIRES. THIS, THEN, IS THE FIFTH REMEDY FOR A LEAN PURSE. OWN THY OWN HOME."

THE SIXTH REMEDY
Insure a Future Income

"The life of every man proceedeth from his childhood to his old age. This is the path of life and no man may deviate from it unless the gods call him prematurely to the world beyond. THEREFORE DO I SAY THAT IT BEHOOVES A MAN TO MAKE PREPARATION FOR A SUITABLE INCOME IN THE DAYS TO COME, WHEN HE IS NO LONGER YOUNG AND TO MAKE PREPARATION FOR HIS FAMILY SHOULD HE BE NO LONGER WITH THEM TO COMFORT AND SUPPORT THEM. This lesson shall instruct thee in providing a full purse when time has made thee less able to earn. So Arkad addressed his class upon the sixth day.

"The man who because of his understanding of the laws of wealth, acquireth a growing surplus, should give thought to those future days. He should plan certain investments or provisions that may endure safely for many years, yet will be available when the time arrives which he has so wisely anticipated.

"There are diverse ways by which a man may provide with safety for his future. He may provide a hiding place and there bury a secret treasure. Yet, no matter with what skill it be hidden it may nevertheless become the loot of thieves. For this reason I recommend not this plan.

"A man may buy houses or lands for this purpose. If wisely chosen, as to their usefulness and value in the future they are permanent in their value and their earnings or their sale will provide well for his purpose.

"A man may loan a small sum to the money lender and increase it at regular periods. The rental which the money lender adds to this will largely add to its increase. I do know a sandal maker named Ansan, who explained to me not long ago that each week for eight years he had deposited with his money lender two pieces of silver. The money lender had but recently given him an accounting over which he greatly rejoiced. The total of his small deposits with their rental at the customary rate of one-fourth their value for each four years, had now become a thousand and forty pieces of silver.

"I did gladly encourage him further by demonstrating to him with my knowledge of the numbers that in twelve years more, if he would keep his regular deposits of but two pieces of silver each week, the money lender would then owe him four thousand pieces of silver, a worthy competence for the rest of his life.

"SURELY WHEN SUCH A SMALL PAYMENT MADE WITH REGULARITY DOTH PRODUCE SUCH PROFITABLE RESULTS NO MAN CAN AFFORD NOT TO INSURE A TREASURE FOR HIS OLD AGE AND THE PROTECTION OF HIS FAMILY, NO MATTER HOW PROSPEROUS HIS BUSINESS AND HIS INVESTMENTS MAY BE.

"I would that I might say more about this. In my mind rests a belief that some day wise-thinking men will devise a plan to insure men against death whereby many men pay in but a trifling sum regularly, the aggregate making a handsome sum for the family of each member who passeth to the beyond. This do I see as something desirable and which I could highly recommend. But today it is not possible because it must reach beyond the life of any man or any partnership to operate. It must be as stable as the king's throne. Some day do I feel that such a plan shall come to pass and be a great blessing to many men, because even the first small payment will make available a snug fortune for the family of a member should he pass on.

"But because we live in our own day and not in the days which are to come, must we take advantage of those means and ways of accomplishing our purposes. Therefore, do I recommend to all men, that they, by wise and well-thought-out methods, do provide against a lean purse in their mature years. For a lean purse to a man no longer able to earn or to a family without its head is a sore tragedy.

"THIS, THEN, IS THE SIXTH REMEDY FOR A LEAN PURSE. PROVIDE IN ADVANCE FOR THE NEEDS OF THY GROWING AGE AND THE PROTECTION OF THY FAMILY."

THE SEVENTH REMEDY
Increase Thy Ability to Earn

"This day do I speak to thee, my students, of one of the most vital remedies for a lean purse. Yet, I will talk not of gold but of yourselves, of the men beneath the robes of many colors who do sit before me. I will talk to you of those things within the minds and lives of men which do work for or against their success." So did Arkad address his class upon the seventh day.

"Not long ago came to me a young man seeking to borrow. When I questioned him the cause of his necessity, he complained that his earnings were insufficient to pay his expenses. Thereupon I explained to him, this being the case, he was a poor customer for the money lender, as he possessed no surplus earning capacity to repay the loan.

"'What you need, young man,' I told him, 'is to earn more coins. What dost thou to increase thy capacity to earn?'

"'All that I can do,' he replied. 'Six times within two moons have I approached my master to request my pay be increased, but without success. No man can go oftener than that.'

"We may smile at his simplicity, yet he did possess one of the vital requirements to increase his earnings. Within him was a strong desire to earn more, a proper and commendable desire.

"PRECEDING ACCOMPLISHMENT MUST BE DESIRE. THY DESIRES MUST BE STRONG AND DEFINITE. General desires are but weak longings. For a man to wish to be rich is of little purpose. For a man to desire five pieces of gold is a tangible desire which he can press to fulfillment. After he has backed his desire for five pieces of gold with strength of purpose to secure it, next he can find similar ways to obtain ten pieces and then twenty pieces and later a thousand pieces and behold, he has become wealthy. In learning to secure his one definite small desire he hath trained himself to secure a larger one. This is the process by which wealth is accumulated; first in small sums, then in larger ones as a man learns and becomes more capable.

"Desires must be simple and definite. They defeat their own purpose should they be too many, too confusing, or beyond the training to accomplish.

"As a man perfecteth himself in his calling even so doth his ability to earn increase. In those days when I was a humble scribe carving upon the clay for a few coppers each day, I observed that other workers did more than I and were paid more. Therefore, did I determine that I would be exceeded by none. Nor did it take long for me to discover the reason for their greater success. More interest in my work, more concentration upon my task, more persistence in my effort, and behold, few men could carve more tablets in a day than I. With reasonable promptness my increased skill was rewarded, nor was it necessary for me to go six times to my master to request recognition.

"The more of wisdom we know, the more we may earn. That man who seeks to learn more of his craft shall be richly rewarded. If he is an artisan, he may seek to learn the methods and the tools of those most skilful in the same line. If he laboreth at the law or at healing, he may consult and exchange knowledge with others of his calling. If he be a merchant, he may continually seek better goods that can be purchased at lower prices.

"Always do the affairs of man change and improve because keen-minded men seek greater skill that they may better serve those upon whose patronage they depend. Therefore, I urge all men to be in the front rank of progress and not to stand still, lest they be left behind.

"Many things come to make a man's life rich with gainful experiences. Such things as the following, a man must do if he shall respect himself:

"HE MUST PAY HIS DEBTS WITH ALL PROMPTNESS WITHIN HIS POWER NOT PURCHASING THAT FOR WHICH HE IS UNABLE TO PAY.

"HE MUST TAKE CARE OF HIS FAMILY THAT THEY MAY THINK AND SPEAK WELL OF HIM.

"HE MUST MAKE A WILL OF RECORD THAT IN CASE THE GODS CALL HIM, PROPER

AND HONORABLE DIVISION OF HIS PROP-
ERTY BE ACCOMPLISHED.

"HE MUST HAVE COMPASSION UPON
THOSE WHO ARE INJURED OR SMITTEN BY
MISFORTUNE AND AID THEM WITHIN REA-
SONABLE LIMITS. HE MUST DO DEEDS OF
THOUGHTFULNESS TO THOSE DEAR TO HIM.

"Thus the seventh and last remedy for a lean purse
is to cultivate thy own powers, to study and become
wiser, to become more skilful, to so act as to respect
thyself. THEREBY SHALT THOU ACQUIRE
CONFIDENCE IN THYSELF TO ACHIEVE THY
CAREFULLY-CONSIDERED DESIRES.

"These, then, are the Seven Remedies for a Lean
Purse, which, out of the experience of a long and successful life I do urge for all men who desire wealth.

"THERE IS MORE GOLD IN BABYLON,
MY STUDENTS, THAN THOU DREAMEST OF.
THERE IS ABUNDANCE FOR ALL.

"GO FORTH AND PRACTICE THESE
TRUTHS THAT THOU MAYEST PROSPER AND
GROW WEALTHY, AS IS THY RIGHT.

"GO THOU FORTH AND TEACH THESE
TRUTHS THAT EVERY HONORABLE SUBJECT
OF HIS MAJESTY MAY ALSO SHARE LIBERALLY

IN THE AMPLE WEALTH OF OUR BELOVED
CITY. THIS IS THY KING'S COMMAND!"

The Treasures
of
Babylon

The Treasures
of Babylon

"A bag heavy with gold or a clay tablet carved with words of wisdom; if thou hadst thy choice, which wouldst thou choose?"

By the flickering light from the fire of desert shrubs, the sun-tanned faces of his listeners gleamed with interest.

"The GOLD, the GOLD," chorused the twenty-seven.

Old Kalabab smiled knowingly.

"Hark," he resumed, raising his hand. "Hear the wild dogs out there in the night. They howl and wail because they are lean with hunger. Yet feed them, and what do they? Fight and strut. Then fight and strut some more, giving no thought to the morrow that will surely come.

"Just so it is with the sons of men. Give them a choice of gold and wisdom—what do they do? Ignore the wisdom and waste the gold. On the morrow they wail because they have no more gold.

"Gold is reserved for those who know its laws and abide by them."

Kalabab drew his white robe close about his lean legs, for a cool night wind was blowing.

"Because thou hast served me faithfully upon our long journey, because thou cared well for my camels, because thou toiled uncomplainingly across the hot sands of the desert, because thou fought bravely the robbers that sought to despoil my merchandise, I will tell thee this night the tale of 'THE FIVE LAWS OF GOLD,' such a tale as thou never hast heard before."

"Hark ye, with deep attention to the words I speak, for if you grasp their meaning and heed them, in the days that come thou shalt have much gold."

He paused impressively. Above in a canopy of blue, the stars shone brightly in the crystal clear skies of Babylonia. Behind the group loomed their faded tents tightly staked against possible desert storms. Beside the tents were neatly stacked bales of merchandise covered with skins. Near by the camel herd sprawled in the sand, some chewing their cuds contentedly, others snoring in hoarse discord.

"Thou hast told us many good tales, Kalabab," spoke up the chief packer. "We look to thy wisdom to guide us upon the morrow when our service with thee shall be at an end."

"I have but told thee of my adventures in strange and distant lands, but this night I shall tell thee of the wisdom of Arkad, the wise rich man."

"Much have we heard of him," acknowledged the chief packer, "for he was the richest man that ever lived in Babylon."

"The richest man he was, and that because he was wise in the ways of gold, even as no man had ever been before him. This night shall I tell of his great wisdom as it was told to me by Nomasir, his son, many years ago in Nineveh, when I was but a lad.

"My master and myself had tarried long into the night in the palace of Nomasir. I had helped my master bring great bundles of fine rugs, each one to be tried by Nomasir until his choice of colors was satisfied. At last he was well pleased and commanded us to sit with him and to drink a rare vintage odorous to the nostrils and most warming to my stomach, which was unaccustomed to such a drink.

"Then, did he tell us this tale of the great wisdom of Arkad, his father, even as I shall tell it to you.

"In Babylon it is the custom, as you know, that the sons of wealthy fathers live with their parents in expectation of inheriting the estate. Arkad did not approve of this custom. Therefore, when Nomasir reached man's estate, he sent for the young man and addressed him:

"'My son, it is my desire that thou succeed to my estate. Thou must, however, first prove that thou art capable of wisely handling it. Therefore, I wish that thou go out into the world and show thy ability both to acquire gold, and to make thyself respected among men.

"'To start thee well, I will give thee two things of which I, myself, was denied when I started as a poor youth to build up a fortune.

"'First, I give thee this bag of gold. If thou use it wisely, it will be the basis of thy future success.

"'Second, I give thee this clay tablet upon which is carved "THE FIVE LAWS OF GOLD." If thou dost but interpret them in thy own acts, they shall bring thee competence and security.

"'Ten years from this day come thou back to the house of thy father and give account of thyself. If thou prove worthy, I will then make thee the heir to my estate. Otherwise, I will give it to the priests that they barter for my soul the kind consideration of the gods.'

"So Nomasir went forth to make his own way, taking his bag of gold, the clay tablet carefully wrapped in silken cloth, his slave and the horses upon which they rode.

"The ten years passed, and Nomasir, as he had agreed, returned to the house of his father, who provided a great feast in his honor, to which he invited many friends and relatives. After the feast was over, the father and mother mounted their throne-like seats at one side of the great hall, and Nomasir stood before them to give an account of himself as he had promised his father.

"It was evening. The room was hazy with smoke from the wicks of the oil lamps that but dimly lighted it. Slaves in white woven jackets and tunics fanned the humid air rhythmically with long-stemmed palm leaves. A stately dignity colored the scene. The wife of Nomasir and his two young sons, with friends and other members of the family, sat upon rugs behind him, eager listeners.

"'My father,' he began deferentially, 'I bow before thy wisdom. Ten years ago when I stood at the gates of manhood, thou bade me go forth and become a man among men, instead of remaining a vassal to thy fortune.

"'Thou gave me liberally of thy gold. Thou gave me liberally of thy wisdom. Of the gold, alas! I must admit of a disastrous handling. It fled, indeed, from my inexperienced hands even as a wild hare flees at the first opportunity from the youth who captures it.'

"The father smiled indulgently. 'Continue, my son, thy tale interests me in all its details.'

"'I decided to go to Nineveh, as it was a growing city, believing that I might find there opportunities. I joined a caravan and among its members made numerous friends. Two well-spoken men who had a most beautiful white horse as fleet as the wind, were among these.

"'As we journeyed, they told me in confidence that in Nineveh was a wealthy man who owned a horse so swift that it had never been beaten. Its owner believed that no horse living could run with greater speed. Therefore, would he wager any sum however large that his horse could outspeed any horse in all Babylonia. Compared to their horse, so my friends said, it was but a lumbering ass that could be beaten with ease.

"'They offered, as a great favor, to permit me to join them in a wager. I was quite carried away with the plan.

"'Our horse was badly beaten and I lost much of my gold.' The father laughed. 'Later I discovered that this was a deceitful plan of these men and they constantly journeyed with caravans seeking victims. You see, the man in Nineveh was their partner and shared with them the bets he won. This shrewd deceit taught me my first lesson in looking out for myself.

"'I was soon to learn another, equally bitter. In the caravan was another young man with whom I became quite friendly. He was the son of wealthy parents and like myself, journeying to Nineveh to find a suitable location. Not long after our arrival, he told me that a merchant had died and his shop with its rich merchandise and patronage could be secured at a paltry price. Saying that we would be equal partners, but first he must return to Babylon to secure his gold, he prevailed upon me to purchase the stock with my gold, agreeing that his would be used later to carry on our venture.

"'He long delayed the trip to Babylon, proving in the meantime to be an unwise buyer and a foolish spender. I finally put him out, but not before the business had deteriorated to where we had only unsaleable goods and no gold to buy other goods. I sacrificed what was left to an Israelite for a pitiful sum.

"'Soon there followed, I tell you, my father, bitter days. I sought employment and found it not, for I was without trade or training that would enable me to earn. I sold my horses. I sold my slave. I sold my extra robes that I might have food and a place to sleep, but each day grim want crouched closer.

"'But in those bitter days, I remembered thy confidence in me, my father. Thou hadst sent me forth to become a man, and this I was determined to accomplish.' The mother buried her face and wept softly.

"'At this time, I bethought me of the tablet thou had given to me upon which thou had carved **"THE FIVE LAWS OF GOLD."** Thereupon, I read most carefully thy words of wisdom, and realized that had I but sought wisdom first, my gold would not have been lost to me. **I learned by heart each law, determined that when once more the goddess of**

good fortune smiled upon me, I would be guided by the wisdom of age and not by the inexperience of youth.

"'For the benefit of you who are seated here this night, I will read the wisdom of my father as engraved upon the clay tablet which he gave to me ten years ago.'

THE FIVE LAWS OF GOLD

1. Gold cometh gladly and in increasing quantity to any man whosoever will put by not less than one tenth of his earnings to create an estate for his future and that of his family.

2. Gold laboreth diligently and contentedly for the wise owner who finds for it profitable employment, multiplying even as the flocks of the field.

3. Gold clingeth to the protection of the cautious owner who invests it under the advice of men wise in its handling.

4. Gold slippeth away from the man who invests it in businesses or purposes with which he is not familiar or which are not approved by those skilled in its keep.

5. Gold flees the man who would force it to impossible earnings or who followeth the alluring

advice of tricksters and schemers or who trusts it to his own inexperience and romantic desires in investment.

"'These are the five laws of gold as written by my father. I do proclaim them as of greater value than gold itself, as I will show by the continuance of my tale.'

"He again faced his father. 'I have told thee of the depth of poverty and despair to which my inexperience brought me.

"'However, there is no chain of disasters that will not come to an end. Mine came when I secured employment managing a crew of slaves working upon the new outer wall of the city.

"'Profiting from my knowledge of the first law of gold, I saved a copper from my first earnings, adding to it at every opportunity until I had a piece of silver. It was a slow procedure, for one must live. I did spend grudgingly, I admit, because I was determined to earn back before the ten years were over, as much gold as you, my Father, had given to me.

"'One day the slave master with whom I had become quite friendly, said to me: 'Thou art a thrifty youth who spends not wantonly what he earns. Hast thou gold put by that is not earning?'

"'Yes,' I replied, 'it is my greatest desire to accumulate gold to replace that which my father gave to me and which I have lost.'

"'Tis a worthy ambition, I will grant, and do you know that the gold which you have saved can work for you and earn much more gold?'

"'Alas! my experience has been bitter, for my father's gold has fled from me, and I am in much fear lest my own do the same.'

"'If thou hast confidence in me, I will give thee a lesson in the profitable handling of gold,' he replied. 'Within a year the outer wall will be complete and ready for the great gates of bronze that will be built at each entrance to protect the city from the king's enemies. In all Nineveh there is not enough metal to make these gates and the king has not thought to provide it. Here is my plan: A group of us will pool our gold and send a caravan to the mines of copper and tin, which are distant, and bring to Nineveh the metal for the gates. When the king says, 'Make the great gates,' we alone can supply the metal and a rich price he will pay. If the king will not buy from us, we will yet have the metal which can be sold for a fair price.'

"'In his offer I recognized an opportunity to abide by the third law and invest my savings under the guidance of wise men. Nor was I disappointed. Our pool was a success, and my small store of gold was greatly increased by the transaction.

"'In due time, I was accepted as a member of this same group in other ventures. They were men wise in the profitable handling of gold. They talked over each plan presented with great care, before entering upon it. They would take no chance on losing their principal or tying it up in unprofitable investments from which their gold could not be recovered. Such foolish things as the horse race and the partnership into which I had entered with my inexperience, would have had scant consideration with them. They would have immediately pointed out their weaknesses.

"'Through my association with these men, I learned to safely invest gold to bring profitable returns. As the years went on, my treasure increased more and more rapidly. I not only made back as much as I lost, but much more.

"'Through my misfortunes, my trials and my success, I have tested time and again the wisdom of the Five Laws of Gold, my father, and have proven them true in every test. **To him who is without knowledge of the Five Laws, Gold comes not**

often, and goeth away quickly. But to him who abideth by the Five Laws, Gold comes and works as his dutiful slave.'

"Nomasir ceased speaking and motioned to a slave in the back of the room. The slave brought forward, one at a time, three heavy leather bags. One of these Nomasir took and placed upon the floor before his father, addressing him again:

"'Thou didst give to me a bag of gold, Babylon gold. Behold in its place, I do return to thee a bag of Nineveh gold of equal weight. An equal exchange as all will agree.

"'Thou didst give to me a clay tablet inscribed with wisdom. Behold, in its stead, I do return two bags of gold.' So saying, he took from the slave the other two bags and, likewise, placed them upon the floor before his father.

"'This I do to prove to thee, my father, of how much greater value I consider thy wisdom than thy gold. Yet, who can measure in bags of gold, the value of wisdom? Without wisdom, gold is quickly lost by those who have it, but with wisdom, gold can be secured by those who have it not, as these three bags of gold do prove.

"'It does, indeed, give to me the deepest satisfaction, my father, to stand before thee and say that, because of thy wisdom, I have been able to become rich and respected before men.'

"The father placed his hand fondly upon the head of Nomasir. 'Thou hast learned well thy lessons, and I am, indeed, fortunate to have a son to whom I may entrust my wealth.'"

Kalabab ceased his tale and looked critically at his listeners.

"What means this to thee, this tale of Nomasir?" he continued.

"Who amongst thee can go to thy father or to the father of thy wife and give an account of wise handling of his earnings?

"What would these venerable men think were you to say, 'I have travelled much and learned much and labored much and earned much, yet alas, of gold I have little. Some I spent wisely, some I spent foolishly and much I lost in unwise ways.'

"Dost still think it but an inconsistency of fate that some men have much gold and others have naught? Then you err.

"Men have much gold when they know the Five Laws of Gold and abide thereby.

"Because I learned these Five Laws in my youth and abided by them, I have become a wealthy merchant. Not by some strange magic did I accumulate my wealth.

"Wealth that comes quickly goeth the same way.

"Wealth that stayeth to give enjoyment and satisfaction to its owner, comes gradually, because it is a child born of knowledge and persistent purpose.

"To earn wealth is but a slight burden upon the thoughtful man. Bearing the burden consistently from year to year accomplishes the final purpose.

"The Five Laws of Gold offer to thee a rich reward for their observance.

"Each of these Five Laws is rich with meaning and lest thou overlook this in the briefness of my tale, I will now repeat them. I do know them each by heart because in my youth, I could see their value and would not be content until I knew them word for word.

The First Law of Gold

Gold cometh gladly and in increasing quantity to any man whosoever will put by not less than one-tenth of his earnings to create an estate for his future and that of his family.

"Any man who will put by one–tenth of his earnings consistently and invest it wisely, will surely create a valuable estate that will provide an income for him in the future and further guarantee safety for his family in case the gods call him to the world of darkness. This law also sayeth that gold cometh gladly to such a man. I can truly certify this in my own life. The more gold I accumulate, the more readily it comes to me and in increased quantities. The gold which I save earns more, even as yours will, and its earnings earn more, and this is the working out of the first law."

The Second Law of Gold

Gold laboreth diligently and contentedly for the wise owner who finds for it profitable employment, multiplying even as the flocks of the field.

"Gold, indeed, is a willing worker. It is ever eager to multiply when opportunity presents itself. To every man who hath a store of gold set by, opportunity comes for its most profitable use. As the years pass, it multiplies itself in surprising fashion."

The Third Law of Gold

Gold clingeth to the protection of the cautious owner who invests it under the advice of men wise in its handling.

"Gold, indeed, clingeth to the cautious owner, even as it flees the careless owner. The man who seeks the advice of men wise in handling gold, soon learneth not to jeopardize his treasure, but to preserve in safety and to enjoy in contentment its consistent increase."

The Fourth Law of Gold

Gold slippeth away from the man who invests it in businesses or purposes with which he is not familiar or which are not approved by those skilled in its keep.

"To the man who hath gold, yet is not skilled in its handling, many uses for it appear most profitable. Too often these are fraught with danger of loss, and if properly analyzed by wise men, show small possibility of profit. Therefore, the inexperienced owner of gold who trusts to his own judgment and invests it in business or purposes with which he is not familiar, too often finds his judgment imperfect, and pays with his treasure for his inexperience.

Wise, indeed, is he who investeth his treasures under the advice of men skilled in the ways of gold."

The Fifth Law of Gold

Gold flees the man who would force it to impossible earnings or who followeth the alluring advice of tricksters and schemers or who trusts it to his own inexperience and romantic desires in its investment.

"Fanciful propositions that thrill like adventure tales always come to the new owner of gold. These appear to endow his treasure with magic powers that will enable it to make impossible earnings. Yet heed ye the wise men for verily they know the risks that lurk behind every plan to make great wealth suddenly.

"Forget not the rich men of Nineveh who would take no chance of losing their principal or tying it up in unprofitable investments.

"This ends my tale of 'The Five Laws of Gold.' In telling it to thee, I have told the secrets of my own success.

"Yet, they are not secrets but truths which every man must first learn and then follow who wishes to step out of the multitude that, like yon wild dogs, must worry each day for food to eat.

"Tomorrow, we enter Babylon. Look! See the fire that burns eternal above the Temple of Bel! We are already in sight of the golden city. Tomorrow, each of thee shall have gold, the gold thou hast so well earned by thy faithful services.

"Ten years from this night, what can you tell about this gold?

"If there be men among you, who, like Nomasir, will use a portion of their gold to start for themselves an estate and be thenceforth wisely guided by the wisdom of Arkad, ten years from now, 'tis a safe wager, like the son of Arkad, they will be rich and respected among men.

"Our wise acts accompany us through life to please us and to help us. Just as surely, our unwise acts follow us to plague and torment us. Alas, they cannot be forgotten. In the front rank of the torments that do follow us, are the memories of the things we should have done, of the opportunities which came to us and we took not.

"Rich are the Treasures of Babylon, so rich no man can count their value in pieces of gold. Each year, they grow richer and more valuable. Like the treasures of every land, they are a reward, a rich reward awaiting those men of purpose who determine to secure their just share.

"In the strength of thine own desires is a magic power. Guide this power with thy knowledge of 'The Five Laws of Gold' and thou shalt share

THE
TREASURES
OF
BABYLON."

The Babylon Course
— in —
Financial
Success

Arranged for Individuals, Families,
Business Executives, Study Groups and Classes

How to Study for
FINANCIAL SUCCESS
By George S. Clason

Who can be successful in acquiring money? Who are the favored ones who can escape the grind of making ends meet and enjoy all the benefits offered by a well-filled purse?

Are they only those with miserly natures, the penny pinchers?

Are they only those born under some lucky star, favorites of the gods?

NOT AT ALL! Financial success is something that is within the reach of every person who has a desire to succeed to such an extent that he is willing to study and work to accomplish his ambition. Financial success is the logical result of consistent effort in the right direction and wisely taking advantage of opportunities even though they be so modest that others ignore them as of no consequence.

Here are the sort of people who are potential fortune-builders—are you among them? Every person who has an income, who draws wages or a salary, who has a profession or who is in business for himself. We must also include every person, even if not employed, who has the ability to hold a position or create profitable employment for himself. Women are as eligible as men. Wives can be of invaluable assistance to their husbands, even when not themselves employed.

And now as to the practical side of fortune building, that most fascinating adventure of all times. There are no mystic secrets to being successful at it. Certain laws—very definite laws—govern our faculty of attracting money to us, our ability to actually acquire money and our knack of being able to keep money. The purpose of "The Babylon Course in Financial Success" is to explain the laws we need to understand to become more successful and to teach ambitious people how to use them to fatten their own purses; to start the student to getting ahead consistently out of their present opportunities and to prepare them to become successful fortune builders in the future.

This course of study is called "The Babylon Course in Financial Success" because we go back to the famous, wealthy city of Babylon for our instructors. Back to Babylon, the wealthiest city of the ancient world, where we become pupils, so to speak, of the wise rich men whose financial genius made their city so extremely wealthy.

Do you desire to learn the knack of getting ahead, that ability to start at financial bedrock, if necessary, and start upward upon the surest and oldest road to financial independence? Are you tired of seeing your hard-earned money slip through your fingers, leaving you always facing that tiresome problem of working just to make ends meet? Would you like to develop within yourself the well-poised ability to carve a success you can be proud of; an ability which will enable you to find success where other men find only failure? Then learn and practise the teachings of this course. Learn them thoroughly and practise them consistently and conscientiously that you may be truly prepared for real success, then you may rest assured that you are on your way to achieve your ambition.

Each lesson is in the form of a tale. Do not be misled by their seeming simplicity into thinking that a casual reading will make you the master of their contents. There is much more to them than at first appears. They appear simple because they deal with basic facts, elementary truths free from confusing complications. The engineers who design the greatest bridges were once little tots in kindergarten where they gained their first insight into straight lines, curves and angles, knowledge that was to be of vital importance in their future successes. Just so, the person who will advance to eminence in building a fortune must so thoroughly learn the basic principles of fortune building that he can use them as instinctively, skilfully and effectively as the bridge engineer uses his knowledge of geometry and mathematics.

Each tale is a composium of practical financial knowledge, knowledge which every student can put right to use to increase his own bank account. Much of this knowledge is self-evident, but the greater part cannot be fully appreciated until the student actually uses it, applies it to his or her own personal finances and sees just how it works and just what results it brings.

Many students experience most valuable results from a first reading. They find at once just the guidance needed to profitably handle some current situation. Therefore they are enabled to make immediate use of what they learn. However, no matter how profitable first results may be, they are but the start. Our lives are more than a month or a year. They normally extend over long periods of years. To the students who thoroughly master the teachings of this course, the wisdom they acquire, will be theirs to guide and help them, not merely for a week or a year, but for all the years of their lives.

PLAN OF STUDY FOR INDIVIDUALS

For individuals who study this course by themselves, the following plan is recommended. First read the lessons, not more than one each day.

When reading them for the first time, try to choose a time when not hurried or liable to interruption. Be fresh and have the mind cleared of other thoughts. In later years, if the purpose of this course is to be fully realized, you will see your financial affairs with their problems and their possibilities, as it were, through the eyes of the wise rich men of ancient Babylon. Therefore, it is essential that your first excursion to the teachers of Babylon find you in the proper frame of mind for your first impressions.

The lessons should be read in the following order:

LESSON No. 1. "The Richest Man in Babylon Tells His System."

LESSON No. 2. "Out of the Ruins of Babylon."

LESSON No. 3. "Seven Remedies for a Lean Purse."

LESSON No. 4. "The Treasures of Babylon."

Each lesson is a part of a definite plan of progressive development for the student. Much of their effectiveness will be lost by hurriedly reading all the lessons or by reading them out of the recommended sequence.

After reading each lesson, do some thinking. See if you can call up examples in your own affairs or in the affairs of other people illustrating the practical working out of the principles explained. If you have had poor luck with money, recall the circumstances in connection with these teachings.

The next step in developing your inherent ability to get ahead is to study each lesson in detail. Allow at least an entire week for each in order that your mind may thoroughly grasp the teachings and do so in a way that will not be forgotten. You should learn these lessons so thoroughly they will become a permanent and practical part of your knowledge. Opportunities will come to you to use this knowledge. The reason for studying it thoroughly is to learn it so well that you will use it instinctively whenever you need it.

To get the full value of the lessons, write out answers to the questions given in the following pages. Make it your task to answer three questions daily. Read the question and look up the reference to the lesson then write out fully an answer. The reading of the entire lesson each day is also recommended while it is being studied.

Also bear in mind that the thoroughness with which you learn the lessons and the readiness with which you can call this knowledge to your aid will mean more dollars in your purse, larger bank balances, greater income, in fact, the start you are seeking to guide you to building a substantial fortune.

The first thorough study of the four lessons should extend over an entire month. Thereafter continue to give thought daily to their teachings. Constantly see how what you have learned will apply to your own financial affairs. The student will be surprised at the rapid development of an ability to analyze and understand financial situations, thus acquiring the faculty of seeing through to the logical conclusion, uninfluenced by emotions, hopes and prejudices. Herein is the basic value of the course, the training of the student to be a logical thinker upon his own finances. Most people, unfortunately, do not progress beyond being financial experimenters. It is the lack of such practical understanding that makes them blunder blindly in vain hopes that illogical conclusions will come to pass.

After concluding the initial study of the course, the student is urged to make a review every six months. This should consist of reading the lessons over, not faster than one each day. Do this re-reading very carefully for you will find in these lessons new ideas and new knowledge because of your own advanced understanding. The more you have learned by practising their teachings, the more additional help they will contain for you.

Many followers of this course have the habit of consulting it whenever they come upon a puzzling situation to handle. They report that it never fails to show a parallel case to theirs or to supply an inspiration for the wise decision they wish to make.

Nor does its help stop at financial problems, the sane, clear thinking men of ancient Babylon supply an inspiration to wise and thoughtful handling of many other situations in personal, family and business relations.

PLAN OF STUDY FOR FAMILIES

Every family has a common interest in the family income. It supplies the family residence and common supply of food and clothing. Also, it is the source from which must come the special requirements of each member, Johnnie's skates, Minnie's Camp Fire outfit, big brother's pocket money, not to mention the needs of father and mother. In most families, the family finances are managed by one of the parents who acts as a friendly despot in apportioning allowances.

This course can do much good in giving all members of a family a true insight into limitations of available money and the advantages of not only living within the family income, but of building up a reserve. It is surprising how much children of even the fourth and fifth grade will learn from these lessons and how willingly they co-operate for the family good when once they understand.

The plan of study recommended is the reading aloud of the lessons and the discussion of the questions. Not only will every member of the family be brought into better harmony on present problems, but they will be securing a basic training for future use.

PLAN OF STUDY FOR BUSINESS EXECUTIVES

The success of every business is dependent upon wise financial management. The volume of sales, quality of products, type of advertising, selection of markets are all secondary in the long run to financial management. The principles of financial advancement taught in this course are basic. They apply just as definitely to the large business as they do to the wage-earner.

These principles should be outstanding in the minds of each executive in a responsible position, to be constantly followed in their private affairs. It is even more important that they be adhered to in planning and operating a business.

Executives of banks and commercial houses find the reading of one of these lessons aloud at the beginning of an executive session, not only arouses interest, but inspires every listener to think how these basic principles can better be adhered to for the enduring prosperity of the institution. In addition to reading the lesson, a few moments given to discussion will lead naturally to considering the applications of the principles taught to the good of the business.

PLAN OF STUDY FOR GROUPS AND CLASSES

The Babylon Course supplies most valuable material for development in class and group study. The lessons should be taken up one at a time in the same sequence as recommended to the individual student. Each member attending should have his own copy of the course.

At the first meeting of the class the first lesson should be read aloud. Then members should be asked to state the impressions created by the lesson thus leading into a general discussion of the entire idea of our personal responsibility for success in acquiring money in amounts larger than our actual requirements for living.

The next meeting should take up the study of specific instances illustrating the teachings of this lesson. Among older students these can come from their own experiences or from the experiences of others with which they may be familiar. Younger students can be advised to consult their parents or other adult friends or relatives. Also, a certain number of the questions on this lesson should be specified for which the students should write out their answers to be discussed at the next meeting.

Each lesson in the course will supply ample material when used in this way for several class lessons. The leader should stimulate the students to think financial problems out for themselves and thus develop the analytical viewpoint and the ability to see through to logical conclusions.

After the entire course has been covered, further study upon each lesson will bring out new illustrations because of the advanced understanding of the class members and their consequent ability to go deeper into the subjects.

QUESTIONS FOR THE STUDENT

The following questions go right to the heart of the basic theme in each lesson. If some of them seem obvious and simple, bear in mind that they are not presented as "puzzlers," but as a practical method of impressing the lessons upon the students' memory.

Therefore the student who wishes to reap the greatest possible financial rewards from studying the course, is urged to look up each reference and write out his answer in detail with all the examples and logic at his command.

LESSON No. I
"The Richest Man in Babylon Tells His System"

This lesson deals with the first basic principle behind success in acquiring money, the right of all persons to keep for themselves a portion of all they earn. Large income is of little advantage except for the temporal pleasures it provides if allowed to go through our hands and leave nothing but memories. A small income judiciously handled may in the end provide much more of satisfaction, enjoyment and worldly possessions than the larger one. As most of us must look to the benefits which an income of moderate proportions can provide, it is essential to our future well-being that we study to become skilfull in handling the resources which we have.

QUESTIONS ON LESSON No. I

1. Explain in more detail the two reasons given by Arkad for the failure of his friends to acquire more than a bare existence from their hard and consistent labors.

2. From your own experience can you cite an example of a person coming into sudden and unearned wealth? If so, tell how it seemed to work out, whether to their permanent financial good or otherwise. If you know of no such example, do you agree with Arkad's opinion? Give your reasons.

3. As a youth, Arkad possessed potential possibilities for financial success. Because he succeeded so much better, should we infer that his friends did not possess similar if not equal potential possibilities? Give your opinion as to what qualities are essential to success with money.

4. As a youth, Arkad was determined to secure a share of the better things of life. Explain the two requisites he considered most essential to doing so.

5. What single rule did Algamish, the money lender, give to Arkad as an initial start on the road to wealth? Can you think of a better one? Give reasons.

6. After making his start as Algamish advised, from what other sources than his earnings was Arkad

advised to build up his financial surplus? Can you cite examples of the results of compound interest over five years, ten, twenty-five?

7. Just when did Algamish advise Arkad to pay himself? Explain why this was the best time.

8. Arkad explains his first investment and how it turned out. Write out a similar fictitious experience for yourself in which you make an investment that turns out the same way. Select modern people and business conditions, but show how the logical conclusion would be similar.

9. Do the same for his second investment as recommended for his first investment in the preceding question.

10. What was Arkad's next error? Transpose this into a modern example in which the advice of Algamish is used.

11. Explain in detail with reasons the three great fundamentals which Arkad learned and which were the basis of his further successes.

12. Why did Arkad disagree with his friend who said it was just luck that Algamish made of him an heir?

13. Explain your own idea upon will power and just what functions it possesses that will aid in achieving financial success.

14. What plan would you recommend to those who desired to get ahead financially and must rely upon their incomes for their start?

15. Did Arkad advise his friends to stint themselves and their families? Do you consider that an average person or family can contract their living expenses 10% without serious inconvenience? What suggestions for so doing can you make?

16. Some of Arkad's questioners realized why Algamish had consistently returned to counsel him. What do you consider the reason or reasons?

17. Just what progress did Arkad need to make before further opportunities opened up for him? Cite how they were similar to the purposes of this pamphlet.

18. Somewhere in his career Arkad made a definite start toward his future successes. At this point he ceased to try merely to make ends meet, because he had a broader and better vision to guide him. State when you think this occurred and why. Do you feel that you have arrived at such a point in your career, have passed it, or are still en route to such a point? Give your reasons.

LESSON No. II
"Out of the Ruins of Babylon"

This lesson considers the question of the obstacles which invariably raise themselves in some way or another between the purposes we wish to accomplish and our means for accomplishing them.

The student who is handicapped by debts that are difficult to liquidate will see herein a practical plan for solving his particular problem. But that is by no means all that the lesson is meant to teach. There can be innumerable other kinds of obstacles to that success which the student is perfectly competent to achieve.

Before answering the following questions the student is urged to take inventory of the obstacles which seem to be retarding his own personal progress to greater financial success. Whatever these obstacles may be, whether debts, responsibility to support others, persons who seem to prevent us from going ahead with our ambitions, or our own personal limitations, environment or lack of opportunity, bear in mind that success is always the reward for overcoming obstacles in some practical way. Success in getting ahead in our money affairs is the logical result of learning to overcome obstacles and becoming capable of making progress in spite of them. After visualizing the obstacles which confront you personally, answer the following questions with this in mind. Write out the answers fully and try to find in your answers suggestions for overcoming the obstacles which may be or seem to be confronting you.

QUESTIONS ON LESSON No. II

1. Give your explanation of the three essentials in the plan which Mathon, the gold lender, suggested to Dabasir whereby he could re-establish himself as a respected citizen of Babylon.

2. Did Mathon's plan take into consideration natural human desires for pleasure and enjoyment or was it a sort of penance for errors. Which should work out to the best advantage in the end?

3. Can you outline a budget for your own earnings that would be consistent with Mathon's plan, allowing you your necessities, shelter, recreation, food, clothing, etc., and still leave for other purposes the proportionate amount which Dabasir was to have to pay off his indebtedness? Try it.

4. In paying off his creditors fairly and honorably would Dabasir pay an equal sum to each, or would he make a division of the amount available so that each debt, regardless of size would

eventually be paid in full in the same number of payments as every other debt? Which would be the fairer way?

5. Do you consider that Dabasir was fundamentally honest and had never had a desire to avoid his just debts? If so, then why had he not tried before to pay these?

6. In this lesson, debts were Dabasir's obstacles. What great truth was it necessary for him to learn before he could overcome his obstacles? Explain how this truth applies to other obstacles.

7. Dabasir's creditors responded differently to his proposed plan of settlement. Do you think their attitude was influenced by their familiarity with his former unreliability? Would a man who had lost his money and gone into debt because of misfortunes other than his own indiscretions have been given more courteous consideration?

8. Explain the factors which kept his courage and his determination to go through with the plan.

9. When business fell off and his earnings shrunk painfully how did Dabasir get by? Did he incur further debts to keep up a standard of living he and his wife had established for themselves? In an emergency do you feel that their way of meeting a temporary embarrassment was justified and wise?

10. In view of the critical attitude of a number of his creditors at first, can you explain the surprising change when he made the final payment? Why should such a tight old chap as Alkahad offer to loan him money after having had so much difficulty in collecting in previous transactions?

11. Dabasir had no regular income to rely upon. The situation of Professor Shrewsbury was different. Explain which of these two was in the most advantageous position to use the plan and why.

12. Professor Shrewsbury's struggles to get even had been in vain before he adopted Mathon's plan. He expressed it as a vicious circle. Explain just how this vicious circle worked.

13. Supposing that debt was not the only obstacle to one's advancement or was not even one of them, do you think it practical to pro-rate one's resources or efforts so as to overcome several obstacles at the same time or would it be wiser to concentrate upon one at a time?

14. What advantages could Shrewsbury offer the merchants to accept the plan? Would any of them have been better off to have refused to accept small payments extending over a long period?

15. Do you think the determination to live upon 70% of their income cost the Shrewsburys severe mental or physical efforts? Did it humiliate

them? Was it an interesting experiment to work out, something like playing a puzzling game?

16. In the position of the Shrewsburys with a portion of your income available for a partial payment investment, one upon which you could pay regularly out of each pay cheque, what type of investment could you recommend that offered these features? First, the sum paid in must be absolutely safe from loss. Second, the accumulated sum must be subject to withdrawal to its full amount. Third, the earnings or interest must be paid at regular periods in cash, or possibly, if you desired, might be left to accumulate. Look up investments available to the small investor which include these features and other desirable ones.

17. After the Shrewsburys had paid off their indebtedness, what use would you suggest for the 20% of their income they had been using for this purpose? Can you suggest a wiser use than that suggested by the professor?

18. In looking at the teachings of this lesson in their broader aspect, in your opinion, what is the outstanding requisite to overcome obstacles? If you feel that there are several requisites of equal importance, name them and explain your reasons.

LESSON No. III
"Seven Remedies For a Lean Purse"

Being successful in acquiring money is, as the student has already learned, dependent upon keeping for ourselves a definite part of our income. It is also dependent upon our determination to succeed, a determination sufficiently firm and deep rooted that we may overcome the obstacles that are almost certain to confront our determinations. But these are not all the requisites to financial success. In addition we must have what can be called a financial programme or a definite plan of action. Once the cards are in our hands we must know how to play them to build up the fortunes we desire.

This lesson outlines for us a definite plan of procedure in our personal and financial affairs, by following which we may carry on our successes to wider and more extensive fields. "The Seven Remedies for a Lean Purse" outlined in this lesson will apply to most of us in the broad principles presented, in that they cover the fundamentals of life. They will also apply with slight variations to business institutions and their operation.

In studying this lesson and in answering the following questions seek for your own use a plan which is practical for you to follow and which will carry you forward to the realization of your own desires and ambitions.

QUESTIONS ON LESSON No. III

1. The situation of need in which Sargon I, King of Babylon, found his people, is similar to the periods of plenty and periods of famine mentioned in Biblical times. Can you cite parallel periods of modern times? In the face of urgent propaganda to spend freely as a help to national prosperity, do you feel that in times of plenty or even moderate plenty we should make provisions for times ahead which may be more difficult? Give reasons based upon your own interests.

2. Did Arkad advise the men attending his class, earning small amounts, to find more profitable work before endeavoring to get ahead? What were his reasons for the advice he gave them?

3. Arkad affirmed that he had little difficulty in getting along upon nine-tenths of his earnings. Take yourself for example. Write out a budget for yourself which calls for you to get along upon nine-tenths of your present average expenditures.

4. In the Second Remedy what unusual fact about the inclination of expenditures in proportion to increased income did Arkad point out? Give your reasons for this.

5. Arkad, although he was the richest man in the richest city in the world, admitted his inability to gratify his every desire. Write out a list of your ungratified desires if you have them. Then divide these into three lists under the following classifications, EASY, DIFFICULT, FANCIFUL. In the first list include those which are quite within your ability and resources if you decide to gratify them. In the second list put those which call for more money, time or effort than you can conveniently give to them or which are difficult because of family or other reasons. On the last list include flights of adventure, romance, travel, etc., that are either impractical or unlikely because of lack of money or opportunity.

This is a very worthwhile method of bringing one's desires into the open and releasing one from suppressions. Consider the first list and decide which are really worth gratifying. Then try to do so deliberately, one at a time. Take it easy, as too many at once detracts from the pleasure. Next consider the second list and make up your mind if any of these would be fully worth the effort required. If so, lay your plans and work for them. For the third list, things that seem impractical, seek a substitute that will gratify your natural longings. In books we can find travel and adventure which will take us upon thrilling mental mental journeys to the far corners of the earth. In study classes we can find mental food and advance ourselves socially and materially. In hobbies we can find wholesome fascinating outlets for our surplus energies. Don't go through life nursing suppressed desires when there are so many worthwhile things within your reach which you can do.

6. In what ways can you adopt Arkad's plan to eliminate unnecessary expenses to your own expenditures?

7. Do you consider a budget just a useless bother or do you agree with Arkad that it is an ally to defend your most cherished desires against less important demands? Give your reasons.

8. Define the difference between hoarding and building up a fortune. What do you think Arkad would have thought about this question?

9. Define your idea of the most satisfactory form of wealth.

10. Explain more fully the three factors Arkad recommended to be considered when making an investment.

11. When making an investment, do you believe in relying entirely upon your own judgment or should you seek the opinions of others? If others, who?

12. Who can be most benefited by owning their own home? Name the advantages.

13. When a part of one's income is being paid upon a home should this sum be considered as necessary living expenses or should it be considered as a permanent saving account and therefore a surplus? Or should a part be apportioned to each?

14. Arkad urges financial protection against unexpected need and against want when one is no longer efficient because of advancing years. Explain what opportunities we enjoy now for financial protection which did not exist in his time. How much protection do you feel that you require and how can you secure it?

15. State the methods Arkad used when he was a scribe to increase his earning capacity and how these methods can be applied to yourself.

16. Do you recognize the universal law of change which is always going on in the affairs of men and believe that for the one who prepares himself to be efficient in any line of endeavor a desirable opportunity will open up? Can you cite an example of one who has progressed because he was ready when opportunity came?

17. Review the four things "a man must do if he is to respect himself" and give your reasons for each.

18. Write out the "Seven Remedies" in a condensed form giving a digest of each. Keep or post in a conspicuous place and read often. Make them a part of your daily thinking that they may continually aid YOUR purse to grow fatter and fatter.

LESSON No. IV
"The Treasures of Babylon"

The road to financial success is not a crooked, wandering trail, but a definite, direct route, the shortest possible way between the point at which we start and the destination we desire to reach.

As normal human beings, we possess many intellectual and emotional characteristics which can sway our actions and influence our decisions. The purpose of this lesson is to implant within the student an understanding of a type of temptations which are bound to come to every person travelling upward on the road to greater financial success. Also to supply them with a method of seeing through these temptations which usually come under one class, opportunities to use one's accumulating capital to make large earnings, in other words, to take short cuts to financial success.

The broad, straight road to success is reasonably safe for the travellers thereon, well-policed, we might say, by the available knowledge of those who have travelled it and are glad to advise others on their way. But there are innumerable, attractive-appearing side roads leading off, which are recommended by advisers with self-interests to promote as shortcuts to wealth, "get-rich-quick" trails, actually, along which the brigands and robbers thrive upon the accumulations of the thrifty.

Of course, the student desires to follow the safe road to success and to avoid errors which could cost his savings. The trap of the "get-rich-quick" is always baited with the illusion of big returns for small investments and the "game" the trapper is after is the investor's capital. In Lesson No. IV will be found "The Five Laws of Gold," which the student is urged to memorize, that, in the future he may wisely judge every opportunity for investing his surplus money and be able to decide upon investments where his capital is safe and can be reclaimed when desired and from which he will receive a fair rate of interest.

QUESTIONS ON LESSON No. IV

1. Nomasir left Babylon and went to a sister city, Nineveh, seeking opportunities. It is an old saying that "Distant fields look greener." In your opinion do you think this idea of going off somewhere to seek opportunity, is wise? Or do you feel that the handicap of being a stranger in a strange land, other things being equal, is a serious disadvantage which must be overcome

before progress can be made? List the advantages of making such a change. List the advantages of staying where you are known and feel at home.

2. Can you explain just how the men in the caravan with the white horse collaborated with the horse owner in Nineveh to fleece travellers? Is this similar to the methods of modern bunko-men who infest railroads, hotels and busy places, seeking acquaintance with strangers carrying money? Can you cite instances coming to your attention through your acquaintances or from reading of such schemes and how they are worked?

3. Can you give an example of a person buying a business they had no previous training for and trying to make it pay? If so, give facts as to how it panned out. If not, what are your opinions of the chances for success of inexperienced people in new businesses?

4. Do you consider that Nomasir took a long chance in going into business with a man he knew only slightly? Can you cite any examples of such partnerships succeeding? Give your ideas of the kind of partnership combinations that might succeed, supposing the people in question were skilful and experienced either in selling, accounting, advertising, manufacturing, management, etc. What are logical combinations for successful co-operation in running a business and what illogical combinations can you name?

5. Can you give reasons why gold seems to come more readily to those who save a part of their earnings or income than to those who can hardly wait to get it before spending? In other words, why do reasonably provident people usually have money, while the improvident are broke and in more or less financial distress a large part of the time? The First Law of Gold.

6. Can you give reasons why gold appears to work so diligently and willingly for some people who not only keep what they have, but enjoy additional revenue from what it earns, while others never derive a satisfactory income from their money? If you believe the way the owners regard their accumulations, has something to do with this, explain how. The Second Law.

7. The idea of gold clinging to anyone may seem fanciful, yet it has a basis of fact. Can you cite an illustration of a person who has gradually built up a substantial estate without appearing to either have a large income, or, on the other hand, appearing to be penurious or short of money? The Third Law.

8. Cite your own experiences with sums of money and state whether it seemed to slip away from you in spite of your desire to keep it. Did you ever try making an investment under the advice of a banker or some party skilled in successfully

handling money who was not personally interested in the investment? How far is it safe to be influenced by the salesman? Do you consider that it is his right to present his proposition, but it is your responsibility to prove the safety of the offer before investing? The Better Business Bureau have a valuable slogan, "Investigate before you invest." The Fourth Law.

9. State, if you can, an example or examples of money "fleeing" from those who were reckless in trusting it to some alluring plan that was to bring very large returns. Can you cite an instance where someone you know made a winning by investing in cheap promotion stocks? From your own knowledge, do speculative investments in intangible propositions, those not backed by market value properties, offer an assurance of profit without serious risk? The Fifth Law.

10. At what point in his career would you say that Nomasir first put his feet on safe financial ground, freed from his impractical ideas about getting rich quick? Explain why.

11. Would you consider the plan of the slave master to buy enough bronze for the city gates as a sound business proposition? State your reasons.

12. If you are acquainted with a group associated to operate a co-operative saving and investment company such as Nomasir joined, state the

advantages in saving, training and earning which they offer to their members. If not acquainted with such a group, state what advantages you feel it would offer to members.

13. Nomasir expresses his opinion of the value of financial wisdom as greater than the value of gold. State your opinion with your reasons.

14. Kalabab states, "Not by some strange magic did I accumulate my wealth." Give your opinion on the harmful influence to individuals of waiting expectantly for "their ship to come in," hoping to find a pot of gold "at the end of the rainbow," and other illusions that some day they will be rich when these ideas are not based upon the results of their own efforts or other tangible propositions of practical value.

15. If you have lost money through an unwise decision or action, do you find the incident inclined to haunt you with unpleasant recollections difficult to forget? If so, write out the incident.

16. Write out a brief statement of any investments or loans you may have made which were unprofitable and state the reasons why. Do the same for profitable loans or investments.

17. Have you ever purposely strengthened your desires as a means of securing their accomplishment? Kalabab states, "In the strength of thine

own desires is a magic power." State whether you feel that concentrating your desires upon success in accumulating and handling money will assist you to be more successful and why.

18. Memorize the "FIVE LAWS OF GOLD." Do this thoroughly so you can repeat them in sequence and can recite each by number without the sequence. Then cultivate the habit of using these as a yard-stick in handling your money as it accumulates. Let them guide you in your decisions. Do not be rushed by decisions based upon desires to take advantage of this or that apparently good opportunity, unless it will stand up under the assay test for merit, under the "Five Laws of Gold."

A PART OF ALL YOU EARN IS YOURS TO KEEP